A Guide to College Partying: Including Keg Stands, Funneling, Kings, Disk Jockeys, Pizza, Homecoming, and More

Annabel Audley

The role of the book within our culture is changing. The change is brought on by new ways to acquire & use content, the rapid dissemination of information and real-time peer collaboration on a global scale. Despite these changes one thing is clear--"the book" in it's traditional form continues to play an important role in learning and communication. The book you are holding in your hands utilizes the unique characteristics of the Internet -- relying on web infrastructure and collaborative tools to share and use resources in keeping with the characteristics of the medium (user-created, defying control, etc.)--while maintaining all the convenience and utility of a real book.

Contents

Articles

Reasons to Party

References

Party Overview

House party

A **house party** in the English-speaking world is typically a type of party where medium to large groups of people gather at a house or apartment of the party's host. The people present at any one party may contain high school, secondary school, college, university students, and/or adults of varying ages, depending on the groups of people concerned. House Parties often nearly always feature food (e.g. buffet) and drink (often alcohol), sometimes music, dancing, as well as general conversation or social interaction (including that of a sexual nature). Consumption of illegal drugs may occur at some parties.

A house party in Denver, Colorado.

Such parties are classified as house parties in order to distinguish them from parties that may take place in college halls of residence and other places on campuses.

Organization

A house party might be organized several months, down to just a few hours, in advance. News of a party is often spread by word of mouth, the sending of formal invitations, or on social networking websites like Facebook. In the case of the latter, the host must be particularly careful of how public the information regarding the party is made. There have been cases where hundreds of people have turned up to a party they found out about on the internet without knowing the host personally, causing massive damage the house or the items within it. In the UK, such an occurrence may be referred to as a 'Skins' party, named after a TV show focusing on the lives of teenagers who often cause such parties.

A person who attends a house party, but is not welcome, is typically referred to as a "gatecrasher".

In some instances house parties do not attract large crowds, and with ten or less people is often referred to as a 'gathering'.

House parties in history

An early example of a house party can be seen in the play *Mostellaria* (*The Haunted House*) by the Roman playwright Plautus. In it a young man called Philolaches is having a great time while his father is away on business.

Sometimes used as a guideline for teenagers in real life, house parties have become a prominent feature in popular movies, particularly movies aimed at teenagers. While many have probably been present before the movie, Animal House is one of the first to properly provide a scene of a House party.

Films containing notable house parties

- *10 Things I Hate about You*
- *American Pie* and *American Pie 2*
- *Animal House*
- *Can't Hardly Wait*
- *Clueless*
- *Coach Carter*
- *Dead Poets Society*
- *Donnie Darko*
- *EuroTrip*
- *Grandma's Boy*
- *House Party, House Party 2, House Party 3*, and *House Party 4: Down to the Last Minute*
- *Kevin & Perry Go Large*
- *Mean Girls*
- *Not Another Teen Movie*
- *Old School*
- *Pretty in Pink*
- *Quadrophenia*
- *Risky Business*
- *Road Trip*
- Sex Drive
- *Scream and Scream 2*
- *Sixteen Candles*
- *Sky High*
- *Some Kind of Wonderful*
- *Speak*
- *Superbad*
- *The New Guy*
- *The Rage: Carrie 2*

- *Uncle Buck*
- *Weird Science*
- *Wild Things 2*

See also

- Cocktail party
- Party
- House Party, Inc.
- Political houseparty
- Art Linkletter's House Party

What to Drink

Distilled beverage

A **distilled beverage**, **liquor**, or **spirit** is a drinkable liquid containing ethanol that is produced by distilling fermented grain, fruit, or vegetables. This excludes undistilled fermented beverages such as beer, wine, and hard cider.

The term **hard liquor** is often used in the United States to distinguish distilled beverages from undistilled ones (implicitly weaker).

Beer and wine are limited to a maximum alcohol content of about 15% ABV, as most yeasts cannot reproduce when the concentration of alcohol is above this level; consequently, fermentation ceases at that point.

The term *spirit* refers to a distilled beverage that contains no added sugar and has at least 20% ABV. Popular spirits include brandy, fruit brandy (also known as eau-de-vie / Schnapps), gin, rum, tequila, vodka, and whisky.

Distilled beverages that are bottled with added sugar and added flavorings, such as Grand Marnier, Frangelico, and American schnapps, are liqueurs.

In common usage, the distinction between spirits and liqueurs is widely unknown or ignored; consequently all alcoholic beverages other than beer and wine are generally referred to simply as *spirits.*

Fortified wines are created by adding a distilled beverage (often brandy) to a wine.

An old whiskey still.

A display of spirits in a supermarket.

Etymology

The origin of "liquor" and its close relative "liquid" was the Latin verb *liquere*, meaning "to be fluid." According to the *Oxford English Dictionary*, an early use of the word in the English language, meaning simply "a liquid," can be dated to 1225. The first use that the OED mentions in reference to a "liquid for drinking" occurred in the early- to mid-14th century. Its use as a term for "an intoxicating alcoholic drink" appeared in the 16th century[citation needed].

The origin of "spirit" in reference to alcohol stems from Middle Eastern alchemy. These alchemists were more involved in medical elixirs than in creating gold from lead. The vapors given off and collected during some of their alchemical processes were described as being the spirits of the original object. When processes akin to distillation were carried out by accident alcohol was produced and the result known as a spirit[citation needed].

History of distillation

Main article: Distillation

Central Asia

Freeze distillation, the "Mongolian still," is known to have been in use in Central Asia sometime in the early Middle Ages. This method involves freezing the alcoholic beverage and removing the ice. The freezing method had limitations in geography and implementation and consequently was not widely used. A notable drawback to this technique is that it concentrates toxins such as methanol and fusel alcohols, rather than reducing concentrations.

Medieval Europe

Although the Greeks and Arabs knew the art of distillation, the earliest written evidence for the distillation of alcohol comes from the School of Salerno in the 12th century. The production method was written in code, suggesting that it was being kept secret. Fractional distillation was developed by Tadeo Alderotti in the 13th century.

In 1437, *burned water* (brandy) was mentioned in the records of the county of Katzenelnbogen in Germany. It was served in a tall, narrow glass called a "goderulffe."

Paracelsus gave alcohol its modern name, taking it from an Arabic word that means "finely divided," in reference to what is done to wine. His test was to burn a spoonful without leaving any residue. Other ways of testing were to burn a cloth soaked in it without actually harming the cloth. In both cases, to achieve this effect the alcohol had to have been at least 95 percent, close to the maximum concentration attainable through distillation (see purification of ethanol).

Claims upon the origin of specific beverages are controversial, often invoking national pride, but they are plausible after the 12th century A.D. when Irish whiskey and German brandy became available.

These spirits would have had a much lower alcohol content (about 40% ABV) than the alchemists' pure distillations, and they were likely first thought of as medicinal elixirs. Consumption of distilled beverages rose dramatically in Europe in and after the mid 14th century, when distilled liquors were commonly used as remedies for the Black Death. Around 1400 it was discovered how to distill spirits from wheat, barley, and rye beers, a cheaper option than grapes. Thus began the "national" drinks of Europe: jenever (Belgium and the Netherlands), gin (England), schnapps (Germany), grappa (Italy), akvavit/snaps (Scandinavia), vodka (Russia and Poland), rakia (the Balkans), poitín (Ireland). The actual names only emerged in the 16th century but the drinks were well known prior to that date.

Modern distillation

The basic process of distillation has not changed since the 8th century. Freeze distillation also remained in limited use, for example during the American colonial period applejack was made from cider using this method.[citation needed] There have been many changes in the methods used to prepare organic material for the still, and the ways the distilled beverage is finished and marketed. Knowledge of the principles of sanitation and access to standardised yeast strains have improved the quality of the base ingredient; larger, more efficient stills produce more product per square foot and reduce waste; ingredients such as corn, rice, and potatoes have been called into service as inexpensive replacements for traditional grains and fruit. For tequila, the blue agave plant is used. Chemists have discovered the scientific principles behind aging, and have devised ways to accelerate aging without introducing harsh flavors. Modern filters have allowed distillers to remove unwanted residue and produce smoother finished products. Most of all, marketing has developed a worldwide market for distilled beverages among populations that previously did not drink spirits.

Microdistilling is a trend that began to develop in the United States following the emergence and immense popularity of microbrewing and craft beer in the last decades of the 20th century. It is specifically differentiated from megadistilleries in the quantity, and arguably quality, of output.

In most jurisdictions, including those that allow unlicensed individuals to make their own beer and wine, it is illegal to distill beverage alcohol without a license—with the notable exception of New Zealand, where personal alcohol distillation is legal (although selling still requires an appropriate licence). Although illegal, moonshining has a long tradition in some locations.

Serving

- Neat or straight — The spirit is served at room temperature without any additional ingredient.
- Straight up — This term refers to an alcoholic drink that is shaken or stirred with ice, strained, and served in a stemmed glass.
- On the rocks — The spirit is served over ice.
- With water.
- With a simple mixer such as club soda, tonic water, juice, or cola.
- As an ingredient of a cocktail.
- With water poured over sugar (as with absinthe)

See also

- Absinthe
- Alcoholic beverage
- Brandy
- Eau-de-vie
- Neutral grain spirit
- Rum
- Schnapps
- Tequila
- Vodka
- Whisky

Bibliography

- Blue, Anthony Dias (2004). *The Complete Book of Spirits: A Guide to Their History, Production, and Enjoyment*. New York: HarperCollins Publishers. p. 324. ISBN 0-06-054218-7.
- Forbes, Robert (1997). *Short History of the Art of Distillation from the Beginnings up to the Death of Cellier Blumenthal*. Brill Academic Publishers. ISBN 90-04-00617-6. (hardcover)
- Multhauf, Robert (1993). *The Origins of Chemistry*. Gordon & Breach Science Publishers. ISBN 2-88124-594-3. (paperback)

External links

- History and Taxonomy of Distilled Spirits. [1]
- Burning Still - Serving the Craft Distilling Community. [2]

Beer

Beer is the world's most widely consumed and probably the oldest of alcoholic beverages; it is the third most popular drink overall, after water and tea. It is produced by the brewing and fermentation of starches, mainly derived from cereal grains—most commonly malted barley, although wheat, maize (corn), and rice are widely used. Most beer is flavoured with hops, which add bitterness and act as a natural preservative, though other flavourings such as herbs or fruit may occasionally be included. Some of humanity's earliest known writings refer to the production and distribution of beer: the Code of Hammurabi included laws regulating beer and beer parlours, and "The Hymn to Ninkasi", a prayer to the Mesopotamian goddess of beer,

Schlenkerla Rauchbier straight from the cask

served as both a prayer and as a method of remembering the recipe for beer in a culture with few literate people. Today, the brewing industry is a global business, consisting of several dominant multinational companies and many thousands of smaller producers ranging from brewpubs to regional breweries.

The basics of brewing beer are shared across national and cultural boundaries. Beers are commonly categorized into two main types—the globally popular pale lagers, and the regionally distinct ales, which are further categorized into other varieties such as pale ale, stout and brown ale. The strength of beer is usually around 4% to 6% alcohol by volume (abv) though may range from less than 1% abv, to over 20% abv in rare cases.

Beer forms part of the culture of beer-drinking nations and is associated with social traditions such as beer festivals, as well as a rich pub culture involving activities like pub crawling and pub games such as bar billiards.

History

Main article: History of beer

Beer is one of the world's oldest prepared beverages, possibly dating back to the early Neolithic or 9000 BC, and is recorded in the written history of ancient Egypt and Mesopotamia. The earliest known chemical evidence of beer dates to circa 3500–3100 BC from the site of Godin Tepe in the Zagros Mountains of western Iran. Some of the earliest Sumerian writings found in the region contain references to a type of beer; one such example, a prayer to the goddess Ninkasi, known as "The Hymn to Ninkasi", served as both a prayer as well as a method of remembering the recipe for beer in a culture with few literate people. The Ebla tablets, discovered

Egyptian wooden model of beer making in ancient Egypt, Rosicrucian Egyptian Museum, San Jose, California

in 1974 in Ebla, Syria and date back to 2,500 BC, reveal that the city produced a range of beers, including one that appears to be named "Ebla" after the city. A beer made from rice, which, unlike sake, didn't use the amylolytic process, and was probably prepared for fermentation by mastication or malting, was made in China around 7,000 BC.

As almost any substance containing carbohydrates, mainly sugars or starch, can naturally undergo fermentation, it is likely that beer-like beverages were independently invented among various cultures throughout the world. The invention of bread and beer has been argued to be responsible for humanity's ability to develop technology and build civilization.

Beer was spread through Europe by Germanic and Celtic tribes as far back as 3000 BC, and it was mainly brewed on a domestic scale. The product that the early Europeans drank might not be recognised as beer by most people today. Alongside the basic starch source, the early European beers might contain fruits, honey, numerous types of plants, spices and other substances such as narcotic herbs. What they did not contain was hops, as that was a later addition first mentioned in Europe around 822 by a Carolingian Abbot and again in 1067 by Abbess Hildegard of Bingen.

Beer produced before the Industrial Revolution continued to be made and sold on a domestic scale, although by the 7th century AD, beer was also being produced and sold by European monasteries. During the Industrial Revolution, the production of beer moved from artisanal manufacture to industrial manufacture, and domestic manufacture ceased to be significant by the end of the 19th century. The development of hydrometers and thermometers changed brewing by allowing the brewer more control of the process and greater knowledge of the results.

Today, the brewing industry is a global business, consisting of several dominant multinational companies and many thousands of smaller producers ranging from brewpubs to regional breweries. As of 2006, more than 133 billion liters (35 billion gallons), the equivalent of a cube 510 metres on a side, of beer are sold per year, producing total global revenues of $294.5 billion (£147.7 billion).

Brewing

Main article: Brewing

A 16th-century brewery

The process of making beer is known as brewing. A dedicated building for the making of beer is called a brewery, though beer can be made in the home and has been for much of its history. A company that makes beer is called either a brewery or a brewing company. Beer made on a domestic scale for non-commercial reasons is classified as homebrewing regardless of where it is made, though most homebrewed beer is made in the home. Brewing beer is subject to legislation and taxation in developed countries, which from the late 19th century largely restricted brewing to a commercial operation only. However, the UK government relaxed legislation in 1963, followed by Australia in 1972 and the USA in 1979, allowing homebrewing to become a popular hobby.

The purpose of brewing is to convert the starch source into a sugary liquid called wort and to convert the wort into the alcoholic beverage known as beer in a fermentation process effected by yeast.

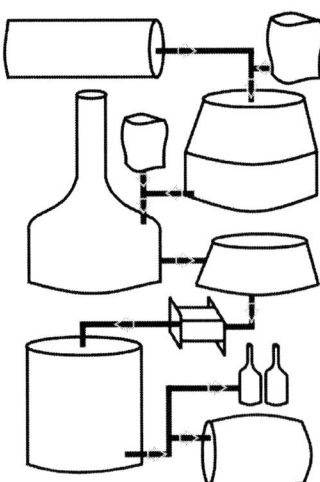

Diagram illustrating the process of brewing beer

Hot Water Tank

Mash Tun

Malt

Hops

Copper

Hopback

Add **Yeast** to

Fermenter

Heat

exchanger

Bottling

Cask or **Keg**

The first step, where the wort is prepared by mixing the starch source (normally malted barley) with hot water, is known as "mashing". Hot water (known as "liquor" in brewing terms) is mixed with crushed malt or malts (known as "grist") in a mash tun. The mashing process takes around 1 to 2 hours, during which the starches are converted to sugars, and then the sweet wort is drained off the grains. The grains are now washed in a process known as "sparging". This washing allows the brewer to gather as much of the fermentable liquid from the grains as possible. The process of filtering the spent grain from the wort and sparge water is called *wort separation*. The traditional process for wort separation is lautering, in which the grain bed itself serves as the filter medium. Some modern breweries prefer the use of filter frames which allow a more finely ground grist. Most modern breweries use a continuous sparge, collecting the original wort and the sparge water together. However, it is possible to collect a second or even third wash with the not quite spent grains as separate batches. Each run would produce a weaker wort and thus a weaker beer. This process is known as second (and third) runnings. Brewing with several runnings is called parti gyle brewing.

The sweet wort collected from sparging is put into a kettle, or "copper", (so called because these vessels were traditionally made from copper) and boiled, usually for about one hour. During boiling, water in the wort evaporates, but the sugars and other components of the wort remain; this allows more efficient use of the starch sources in the beer. Boiling also destroys any remaining enzymes left over from the mashing stage. Hops are added during boiling as a source of bitterness, flavour and aroma. Hops may be added at more than one point during the boil. The longer the hops are boiled, the more bitterness they contribute, but the less hop flavour and aroma remains in the beer.

After boiling, the hopped wort is now cooled, ready for the yeast. In some breweries, the hopped wort may pass through a hopback, which is a small vat filled with hops, to add aromatic hop flavouring and to act as a filter; but usually the hopped wort is simply cooled for the fermenter, where the yeast is added. During fermentation, the wort becomes beer in a process which requires a week to months depending on the type of yeast and strength of the beer. In addition to producing alcohol, fine particulate matter suspended in the wort settles during fermentation. Once fermentation is complete, the yeast also settles, leaving the beer clear.

Fermentation is sometimes carried out in two stages, primary and secondary. Once most of the alcohol has been produced during primary fermentation, the beer is transferred to a new vessel and allowed a period of secondary fermentation. Secondary fermentation is used when the beer requires long storage before packaging or greater clarity. When the beer has fermented, it is packaged either into casks for cask ale or kegs, aluminium cans, or bottles for other sorts of beer.

Ingredients

The basic ingredients of beer are water; a starch source, such as malted barley, able to be fermented (converted into alcohol); a brewer's yeast to produce the fermentation; and a flavouring such as hops. A mixture of starch sources may be used, with a secondary starch source, such as maize (corn), rice or sugar, often being termed an adjunct, especially when used as a lower-cost substitute for malted barley. Less widely used starch sources include millet, sorghum and cassava root in Africa, potato in Brazil, and agave in Mexico, among others. The amount of each starch source in a beer recipe is collectively called the grain bill.

Malted barley before roasting

Water

Beer is composed mostly of water. Regions have water with different mineral components; as a result, different regions were originally better suited to making certain types of beer, thus giving them a regional character. For example, Dublin has hard water well suited to making stout, such as Guinness; while Pilzen has soft water well suited to making pale lager, such as Pilsner Urquell. The waters of Burton in England contain gypsum, which benefits making pale ale to such a degree that brewers of pale ales will add gypsum to the local water in a process known as Burtonisation.

Starch source

Main articles: Malt and Mash ingredients

The starch source in a beer provides the fermentable material and is a key determinant of the strength and flavour of the beer. The most common starch source used in beer is malted grain. Grain is malted by soaking it in water, allowing it to begin germination, and then drying the partially germinated grain in a kiln. Malting grain produces enzymes that convert starches in the grain into fermentable sugars. Different roasting times and temperatures are used to produce different colours of malt from the same grain. Darker malts will produce darker beers.

Nearly all beer includes barley malt as the majority of the starch. This is because of its fibrous husk, which is not only important in the sparging stage of brewing (in which water is washed over the mashed barley grains to form the wort), but also as a rich source of amylase, a digestive enzyme which facilitates conversion of starch into sugars. Other malted and unmalted grains (including wheat, rice, oats, and rye, and less frequently, corn and sorghum) may be used. In recent years, a few brewers have produced gluten-free beer made with sorghum with no barley malt for those who cannot consume gluten-containing grains like wheat, barley, and rye.

Hops

Main article: Hops

Flavouring beer is the sole major commercial use of hops. The flower of the hop vine is used as a flavouring and preservative agent in nearly all beer made today. The flowers themselves are often called "hops".

Hop cone in a Hallertau, Germany, hop yard

Hops were used by monastery breweries, such as Corvey in Westphalia, Germany, from AD 822, though the date normally given for widespread cultivation of hops for use in beer is the thirteenth century. Before the thirteenth century, and until the sixteenth century, during which hops took over as the dominant flavouring, beer was flavoured with other plants; for instance, *Glechoma hederacea*. Combinations of various aromatic herbs, berries, and even ingredients like wormwood would be combined into a mixture known as gruit and used as hops are now used. Some beers today, such as Fraoch' by the Scottish Heather Ales company and Cervoise Lancelot by the French Brasserie-Lancelot company, use plants other than hops for flavouring.

Hops contain several characteristics that brewers desire in beer. Hops contribute a bitterness that balances the sweetness of the malt; the bitterness of beers is measured on the International Bitterness Units scale. Hops contribute floral, citrus, and herbal aromas and flavours to beer. Hops have an antibiotic effect that favours the activity of brewer's yeast over less desirable microorganisms, and hops aids in "head retention", the length of time that a foamy head created by carbonation will last. The acidity of hops is a preservative.

Yeast

Main articles: Brewer's yeast, Saccharomyces cerevisiae, and Saccharomyces uvarum

Yeast is the microorganism that is responsible for fermentation in beer. Yeast metabolises the sugars extracted from grains, which produces alcohol and carbon dioxide, and thereby turns wort into beer. In addition to fermenting the beer, yeast influences the character and flavour. The dominant types of yeast used to make beer are ale yeast (*Saccharomyces cerevisiae*) and lager yeast (*Saccharomyces uvarum*); their use distinguishes ale and lager. *Brettanomyces* ferments lambics, and *Torulaspora delbrueckii* ferments Bavarian weissbier. Before the role of yeast in fermentation was understood, fermentation involved wild or airborne yeasts. A few styles such as lambics rely on this method today, but most modern fermentation adds pure yeast cultures.

Clarifying agent

Main article: Finings

Some brewers add one or more clarifying agents to beer, which typically precipitate (collect as a solid) out of the beer along with protein solids and are found only in trace amounts in the finished product. This process makes the beer appear bright and clean, rather than the cloudy appearance of ethnic and older styles of beer such as wheat beers.

Examples of clarifying agents include isinglass, obtained from swimbladders of fish; Irish moss, a seaweed; kappa carrageenan, from the seaweed *Kappaphycus cottonii*; Polyclar (artificial); and gelatin. If a beer is marked "suitable for Vegans", it was clarified either with seaweed or with artificial agents.

See also: Vegetarianism and beer

Production

The brewing industry is a global business, consisting of several dominant multinational companies and many thousands of smaller producers ranging from brewpubs to regional breweries. More than 133 billion liters (35 billion gallons) are sold per year—producing total global revenues of $294.5 billion (£147.7 billion) in 2006.

Cropton, a typical UK microbrewery

A microbrewery, or craft brewery, is a modern brewery which produces a limited amount of beer. The maximum amount of beer a brewery can produce and still be classed as a microbrewery varies by region and by authority, though is usually around 15,000 barrels (18,000 hectolitres/ 475,000 US gallons) a year. A brewpub is a type of microbrewery that incorporates a pub or other eating establishment.

SABMiller became the largest brewing company in the world when it acquired Royal Grolsch, brewer of Dutch premium beer brand Grolsch. InBev was the second-largest beer-producing company in the world, and Anheuser-Busch held the third spot, but after the merger between InBev and Anheuser-Busch, the new Anheuser-Busch InBev company is the largest brewer in the world.

Brewing at home is subject to regulation and prohibition in many countries. Restrictions on homebrewing were lifted in the UK in 1963, Australia followed suit in 1972, and the USA in 1978, though individual states were allowed to pass their own laws limiting production.

Varieties

Main article: Beer style

While there are many types of beer brewed, the basics of brewing beer are shared across national and cultural boundaries. The traditional European brewing regions—Germany, Belgium, the United Kingdom, Ireland, Poland, the Czech Republic, Scandinavia, the Netherlands and Austria—have local varieties of beer. In some countries, notably the USA, Canada, and Australia, brewers have adapted European styles to such an extent that they have effectively created their own indigenous types.

Kriek, a variety of beer brewed with cherries

Despite the regional variations, beer is categorised into two main types based on the temperature of the brewing which influences the behaviour of yeast used during the brewing process—lagers, which are brewed at a low temperature, and the more regionally distinct ales, brewed at a higher temperature. Ales are further categorised into other varieties such as pale ale, brown or dark ale, and stout.

Michael Jackson, in his 1977 book *The World Guide To Beer*, categorised beers from around the world in local style groups suggested by local customs and names. Fred Eckhardt furthered Jackson's work in *The Essentials of Beer Style* in 1989.

The most common method of categorising beer is by the behaviour of the yeast used in the fermentation process. Beers using a fast acting warm fermentation which leaves behind residual sugars are termed "ales", while beers using a slower-acting cool fermentation, with a yeast which removes most of the sugars, producing a clean, dry beer, are termed "lagers". Differences between some ales and lagers can be difficult to categorise. Steam beer, Kölsch, Alt, and some modern British Golden Summer Beers use elements of both lager and ale production. Baltic Porter and Bière de Garde may be produced by either lager or ale methods or a combination of both. However, lager production results in a cleaner-tasting, drier and lighter beer than ale.

Lambic

Lambic, a beer of Belgium, is naturally fermented using wild yeasts, rather than cultivated. Many of these are not strains of brewer's yeast (*Saccharomyces cerevisiae*) and may have significant differences in aroma and sourness. Yeast varieties such as *Brettanomyces bruxellensis* and *Brettanomyces lambicus* are common in lambics. In addition, other organisms such as Lactobacillus bacteria produce acids which contribute to the sourness.

Stout

Stout and porter are dark beers made using roasted malts or roast barley, and typically brewed with slow fermenting yeast. There are a number of variations including Baltic porter, dry stout, and Imperial stout. The name Porter was first used in 1721 to describe a dark brown beer popular with the street and river porters of London. This same beer later also became known as stout, though the word stout had been used as early as 1677. The history and development of stout and porter are intertwined.

Wheat

Wheat beer is brewed with a large proportion of wheat although it often also contains a significant proportion of malted barley. Wheat beers are usually top-fermented (in Germany they have to be by law). The flavour of wheat beers varies considerably, depending upon the specific style.

Ale

Main article: Ale

Cask ale hand pumps with pump clips detailing the beers and their breweries

Ales are normally brewed using a warm fermentation, and a strain of brewers' yeast (most commonly *Saccharomyces cerevisiae*) that clumps and rises to the surface; because of this they are often referred to as "top cropping" or "top fermenting"— though this distinction is less clear in modern brewing with the use of cylindro-conical tanks, where the behaviour of lager and ale yeast are quite similar. The important distinction for ales is that they are fermented at higher temperatures and thus ferment more quickly than lagers.

Ale is typically fermented at temperatures between 15 and 24°C (60 and 75°F). At these temperatures, yeast produces significant amounts of esters and other secondary flavour and aroma products, and the result is often a beer with slightly "fruity" compounds resembling apple, pear, pineapple, banana, plum, or prune, among others.

Before the introduction of hops into England from the Netherlands in the 15th century, the name "ale" was exclusively applied to unhopped fermented beverages, the term *beer* being gradually introduced to describe a brew with an infusion of hops. This distinction no longer applies. The word *ale* may come from the Old English *ealu*, in turn from the Proto-Indo-European base *alut-*, which holds connotations of "sorcery, magic, possession, intoxication".

Real ale is the term coined by the Campaign for Real Ale (CAMRA) in 1973 for "beer brewed from traditional ingredients, matured by secondary fermentation in the container from which it is dispensed, and served without the use of extraneous carbon dioxide". It is applied to bottle conditioned and cask conditioned beers.

Lager

Main article: Lager

Lager is the English name for cool fermenting beers of Central European origin. Pale lagers are the most commonly consumed beers in the world. The name "lager" comes from the German "lagern" for "to store", as brewers around Bavaria stored beer in cool cellars and caves during the warm summer months. These brewers noticed that the beers continued to ferment, and to also clear of sediment, when stored in cool conditions.

Lager yeast is a cool bottom-fermenting yeast (*Saccharomyces pastorianus*) and typically undergoes primary fermentation at 7–12 °C (45–54 °F) (the fermentation phase), and then is given a long secondary fermentation at 0–4 °C (32–39 °F) (the lagering phase). During the secondary stage, the lager clears and mellows. The cooler conditions also inhibit the natural production of esters and other byproducts, resulting in a "cleaner"-tasting beer.

Modern methods of producing lager were pioneered by Gabriel Sedlmayr the Younger, who perfected dark brown lagers at the Spaten Brewery in Bavaria, and Anton Dreher, who began brewing a lager (now known as Vienna lager), probably of amber-red colour, in Vienna in 1840–1841. With improved modern yeast strains, most lager breweries use only short periods of cold storage, typically 1–3 weeks.

Measurement

Main article: Beer measurement

Beer is measured and assessed by bitterness, by strength and by colour. The perceived bitterness is measured by the International Bitterness Units scale (IBU), defined in co-operation between the American Society of Brewing Chemists and the European Brewery Convention. The international scale was a development of the European Bitterness Units scale, often abbreviated as EBU, and the bitterness values should be identical.

Colour

Beer colour is determined by the malt. The most common colour is a pale amber produced from using pale malts. *Pale lager* and *pale ale* are terms used for beers made from malt dried with coke. Coke was first used for roasting malt in 1642, but it was not until around 1703 that the term *pale ale* was used.

Paulaner dunkel - a dark lager

In terms of sales volume, most of today's beer is based on the pale lager brewed in 1842 in the town of Pilsen in the present-day Czech Republic. The modern pale lager is light in colour with a noticeable carbonation (fizzy bubbles) and a typical alcohol by volume content of around 5%. The Pilsner Urquell, Bitburger, and Heineken brands of beer are typical examples of pale lager, as are the American brands Budweiser, Coors, and Miller.

Dark beers are usually brewed from a pale malt or lager malt base with a small proportion of darker malt added to achieve the desired shade. Other colourants—such as caramel—are also widely used to darken beers. Very dark beers, such as stout, use dark or patent malts that have been roasted longer. Some have roasted unmalted barley.

Strength

See also: Beer measurement#By strength

Beer ranges from less than 3% alcohol by volume (abv) to around 14% abv, though this strength can be increased to around 20% by re-pitching with champagne yeast, and to 55% abv by the freeze-distilling process. The alcohol content of beer varies by local practice or beer style. The pale lagers that most consumers are familiar with fall in the range of 4–6%, with a typical abv of 5%. The customary strength of British ales is quite low, with many session beers being around 4% abv. Some beers, such as table beer are of such low alcohol content (1%–4%) that they are served instead of soft drinks in some schools.

The alcohol in beer comes primarily from the metabolism of sugars that are produced during fermentation. The quantity of fermentable sugars in the wort and the variety of yeast used to ferment the wort are the primary factors that determine the amount of alcohol in the final beer. Additional fermentable sugars are sometimes added to increase alcohol content, and enzymes are often added to the wort for certain styles of beer (primarily "light" beers) to convert more complex carbohydrates (starches) to fermentable sugars. Alcohol is a by-product of yeast metabolism and is toxic to the yeast; typical brewing yeast cannot survive at alcohol concentrations above 12% by volume. Low temperatures and too little fermentation time decreases the effectiveness of yeasts and consequently decreases the alcohol content.

Exceptionally strong beers

The strength of beers has climbed during the later years of the 20th century. Vetter 33, a 10.5% abv (33 degrees Plato, hence Vetter "33") doppelbock, was listed in the 1994 *Guinness Book of World Records* as the strongest beer at that time, though Samichlaus, by the Swiss brewer Hürlimann, had also been listed by the *Guinness Book of World Records* as the strongest at 14% abv. Since then, some brewers have used champagne yeasts to increase the alcohol content of their beers. Samuel Adams reached 20% abv with *Millennium*, and then surpassed that amount to 25.6% abv with Utopias. The strongest beer brewed in Britain was Baz's Super Brew by Parish Brewery, a 23% abv beer.

The product that is claimed to be the strongest beer made is *The End of History*, a 55% Belgian ale, made by the Scottish brewery BrewDog in 2010, who also made *Sink The Bismarck!*, a 41% abv IPA, and *Tactical Nuclear Penguin*, a 32% abv Imperial Stout; these are made using the eisbock method of freeze distilling in which the brewery freeze distils a strong ale, gradually removing the ice and freezing again until the beer reaches the strength required, a process that may class the finished products as spirits rather than beer. The German brewery Schorschbräu's *Schorschbock*—a 31% abv eisbock, and Hair of the Dog's *Dave*—a 29% abv barley wine made in 1994, both used the same freeze distilling method. A 60% abv blend of beer with whiskey was jokily claimed as the strongest beer by a Dutch brewery in July 2010.

Serving

Draught

Main articles: Draught beer, Keg beer, and Cask ale

Draught beer from a pressurised keg is the most common method of dispensing in bars around the world. A metal keg is pressurised with carbon dioxide (CO_2) gas which drives the beer to the dispensing tap or faucet. Some beers may be served with a nitrogen/carbon dioxide mixture. Nitrogen produces fine bubbles, resulting in a dense head and a creamy mouthfeel. Some types of beer can also be found in smaller, disposable kegs called beer balls.

Draught beer keg fonts at the Délirium Café in Brussels

In the 1980s, Guinness introduced the beer widget, a nitrogen-pressurised ball inside a can which creates a dense, tight head, similar to beer served from a nitrogen system. The words *draft* and *draught* can be used as marketing terms to describe canned or bottled beers containing a beer widget, or which are cold-filtered rather than pasteurised.

A selection of cask beers

Cask-conditioned ales (or cask ales) are unfiltered and unpasteurised beers. These beers are termed "real ale" by the CAMRA organisation. Typically, when a cask arrives in a pub, it is placed horizontally on a frame called a "stillage" which is designed to hold it steady and at the right angle, and then allowed to cool to cellar temperature (typically between 12–14 °C / 54–57 °F), before being tapped and vented—a tap is driven through a (usually rubber) bung at the bottom of one end, and a hard spile or other implement is used to open a hole in the side of the cask, which is now uppermost. The act of stillaging and then venting a beer in this manner typically disturbs all the sediment, so it must be left for a suitable period to "drop" (clear) again, as well as to fully condition—this period can take anywhere from several hours to several days. At this point the beer is ready to sell, either being pulled through a beer line with a hand pump, or simply being "gravity-fed" directly into the glass.

Draught beer's environmental impact can be 68% lower than bottled beer due to packaging differences. Home brewing can reduce the environmental impact of beer via less packaging and transportation. A life cycle study of one beer brand, including grain production, brewing, bottling, distribution and waste management, shows that the CO_2 emissions from a 6-pack of micro-brew beer is about 3 kilograms (6.6 pounds). The loss of natural habitat potential from the 6-pack of micro-brew beer is estimated to be 2.5 square meters (26 square feet). Downstream emissions from distribution, retail, storage and disposal of waste can be over 45% of a bottled micro-brew beer's CO_2 emissions. Where legal, the use of a refillable jug, reusable bottle or other reusable containers to transport draught beer from a store or a bar, rather than buying pre-bottled beer, can reduce the environmental impact of beer consumption.

Packaging

Main articles: Beer bottle and Beverage can

Most beers are cleared of yeast by filtering when packaged in bottles and cans. However, bottle conditioned beers retain some yeast—either by being unfiltered, or by being filtered and then reseeded with fresh yeast. It is usually recommended that the beer be poured slowly, leaving any yeast sediment at the bottom of the bottle. However, some drinkers prefer to pour in the yeast; this practice is customary with wheat beers. Typically, when serving a hefeweizen, 90% of the contents are poured, and the remainder is swirled to suspend the sediment before pouring it into the glass. Alternatively, the bottle may be inverted prior to opening. Glass bottles are always used for bottle conditioned beers.

A beer can with the Wikipedia logo

Many beers are sold in cans, though there is considerable variation in the proportion between different countries. In Sweden in 2001, 63.9% of beer was sold in cans. People either drink from the can or pour the beer into a glass. Cans protect the beer from light (thereby preventing "skunked" beer) and have a seal less prone to leaking over time than bottles. Cans were initially viewed as a technological breakthrough for maintaining the quality of a beer, then became commonly associated with less expensive, mass-produced beers, even though the quality of storage in cans is much like bottles. Plastic (PET) bottles are used by some breweries.

Temperature

Édouard Manet's *The Waitress* showing a woman serving beer

The temperature of a beer has an influence on a drinker's experience; warmer temperatures reveal the range of flavours in a beer but cooler temperatures are more refreshing. Most drinkers prefer pale lager to be served chilled, a low- or medium-strength pale ale to be served cool, while a strong barley wine or imperial stout to be served at room temperature.

Beer writer Michael Jackson proposed a five-level scale for serving temperatures: well chilled (7 °C/45 °F) for "light" beers (pale lagers); chilled (8 °C/46 °F) for Berliner Weisse and other wheat beers; lightly chilled (9 °C/48 °F) for all dark lagers, altbier and German wheat beers; cellar temperature (13 °C/55 °F) for regular British ale, stout and most Belgian specialities; and room temperature (15.5 °C/59.9 °F) for strong dark ales (especially trappist beer) and barley wine.

Drinking chilled beer began with the development of artificial refrigeration and by the 1870s, was spread in those countries that concentrated on brewing pale lager. Chilling beer makes it more refreshing, though below 15.5 °C (59.9 °F) the chilling starts to reduce taste awareness and reduces it significantly below 10 °C (50 °F). Beer served unchilled—either cool or at room temperature, reveal more of their flavours. Cask Marque, a non-profit UK beer organisation, has set a temperature standard range of 12°-14 °C (53°-57 °F) for cask ales to be served.

Vessels

Main article: Beer glassware

Beer is consumed out of a variety of vessels, such as a glass, a beer stein, a mug, a pewter tankard, a beer bottle or a can. The shape of the glass from which beer is consumed can influence the perception of the beer and can define and accent the character of the style. Breweries offer branded glassware intended only for their own beers as a marketing promotion, as this increases sales.

The pouring process has an influence on a beer's presentation. The rate of flow from the tap or other serving vessel, tilt of the glass, and position of the pour (in the centre or down the side) into the glass all influence the end result, such as the size and longevity of the head, lacing (the pattern left by the head as it moves down the glass as the beer is drunk), and turbulence of the beer and its release of carbonation.

Beer and society

See also: Category:Beer culture

Various social traditions and activities are associated with beer drinking, such as playing cards, darts, or other pub games; attending beer festivals, or visiting a series of different pubs in one evening; joining an organisation such as CAMRA; or rating beer. Various drinking games, such as beer pong, are also popular.

A tent at Munich's Oktoberfest—the world's largest beer festival

Beer is considered to be a social lubricant in many societies, and is consumed in countries all over the world. There are breweries in Middle Eastern countries such as Iran, and Syria, as well as African countries. Sales of beer are four times that of wine, the second most popular alcoholic beverage. In Russia, consumption is on the rise as younger generations are choosing beer over vodka. In most societies, beer is the most popular alcoholic beverage.

Health effects

The main active ingredient of beer is alcohol, and therefore, the health effects of alcohol apply to beer. The moderate consumption of alcohol, including beer, is associated with a decreased risk of cardiac disease, stroke and cognitive decline. The long-term effects of alcohol abuse, however, include the risk of developing alcoholism and alcoholic liver disease.

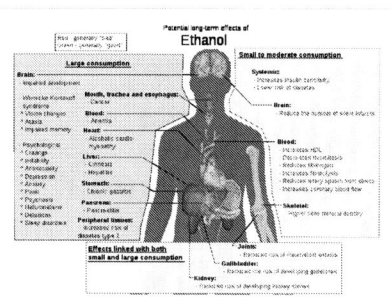

Overview of possible long-term effects of ethanol. Click to enlarge.

Brewer's yeast is known to be a rich source of nutrients; therefore, as expected, beer can contain significant amounts of nutrients, including magnesium, selenium, potassium, phosphorus, biotin, and B vitamins. In fact, beer is sometimes referred to as "liquid bread". Some sources maintain that filtered beer loses much of its nutrition.

A 2005 Japanese study found that low alcohol beer may possess strong anti-cancer properties. Another study found nonalcoholic beer to mirror the cardiovascular benefits associated with moderate consumption of alcoholic beverages.

However, much research suggests that the primary health benefit from alcoholic beverages comes from the alcohol they contain.

It is considered that overeating and lack of muscle tone is the main cause of a beer belly, rather than beer consumption. A recent study, however, found a link between binge drinking and a beer belly. But with most overconsumption, it is more a problem of improper exercise and overconsumption of carbohydrates than the product itself. Several diet books quote beer as having an undesirably high glycemic index of 110, the same as maltose; however, the maltose in beer undergoes metabolism by yeast during fermentation so that beer consists mostly of water, hop oils and only trace amounts of sugars, including maltose.

Related beverages

See also: Category:Types of beer

Around the world, there are a number of traditional and ancient starch-based beverages classed as beer. In Africa, there are various ethnic beers made from sorghum or millet, such as Oshikundu in Namibia and Tella in Ethiopia. Kyrgyzstan also has a beer made from millet; it is a low alcohol, somewhat porridge-like drink called "Bozo". Bhutan, Nepal, Tibet and Sikkim also use millet in Chhaang, a popular semi-fermented rice/millet drink in the eastern Himalayas. Further east in China are found Huangjiu and Choujiu—traditional rice-based beverages related to beer.

The Andes in South America has Chicha, made from germinated maize (corn); while the indigenous peoples in Brazil have Cauim, a traditional beverage made since pre-Columbian times by chewing manioc so that enzymes present in human saliva can break down the starch into fermentable sugars;

this is similar to Masato in Peru.

Some beers which are made from bread, which is linked to the earliest forms of beer, are Sahti in Finland, Kvass in Russia and the Ukraine, and Bouza in Sudan.

Bibliography

- Dumper, Michael; Stanley, Bruce E. (2007). *Cities of the Middle East and North Africa: A Historical Encyclopedia* [1]. ABC-CLIO. ISBN 9781576079195.
- *Archeological Parameters For the Origins of Beer* [2]. Thomas W. Kavanagh.
- *The Complete Guide to World Beer*, Roger Protz. ISBN 1-84442-865-6.
- *The Barbarian's Beverage: a history of beer in ancient Europe*, Max Nelson. ISBN 0-415-31121-7.
- *The World Guide to Beer*, Michael Jackson. ISBN 1-85076-000-4
- *The New World Guide to Beer*, Michael Jackson. ISBN 0-89471-884-3
- *Beer: The Story of the Pint*, Martyn Cornell. ISBN 0-7553-1165-5
- *Beer and Britannia: An Inebriated History of Britain*, Peter Haydon. ISBN 0-7509-2748-8
- *The Book of Beer Knowledge: Essential Wisdom for the Discerning Drinker, a Useful Miscellany*, Jeff Evans. ISBN 1-85249-198-1
- *Country House Brewing in England, 1500–1900*, Pamela Sambrook. ISBN 1-85285-127-9
- *Ale, Beer and Brewsters in England: Women's Work in a Changing World, 1300–1600* , Judith M. Bennett. ISBN 0-19-512650-5
- *A History of Beer and Brewing*, I. Hornsey. ISBN 0-85404-630-5
- *Beer: an Illustrated History*, Brian Glover. ISBN 1-84038-597-9
- *Beer in America: The Early Years 1587–1840—Beer's Role in the Settling of America and the Birth of a Nation*, Gregg Smith. ISBN 0-937381-65-9
- *Big Book of Beer*, Adrian Tierney-Jones. ISBN 1-85249-212-0
- *Gone for a Burton: Memories from a Great British Heritage*, Bob Ricketts. ISBN 1-905203-69-1
- *Farmhouse Ales: Culture and Craftsmanship in the Belgian Tradition*, Phil Marowski. ISBN 0-937381-84-5
- *The World Encyclopedia of Beer*, Brian Glover. ISBN 0-7548-0933-1
- *The Complete Joy of Homebrewing*, Charlie Papazian ISBN 0-380-77287-6 (This is the seminal work on home brewing that is almost universally suggested to new hobbyist)
- *The Brewmaster's Table*, Garrett Oliver. ISBN 0-06-000571-8
- Vaughan, J. G.; C. A. Geissler (1997). *The New Oxford Book of Food Plants*. Oxford University Press. ISBN 0-19-854825-7.
- *Bacchus and Civic Order: The Culture of Drink in Early Modern Germany*, Ann Tlusty. ISBN 0-8139-2045-0

krc:Сыра pnb:ری pcd:Biére

Wine

Wine glasses of white (left) and red wines(right).

Wine is an alcoholic beverage, typically made of fermented grape juice. The natural chemical balance of grapes is such that they can ferment without the addition of sugars, acids, enzymes or other nutrients. Wine is produced by fermenting crushed grapes using various types of yeast. Yeast consumes the sugars found in the grapes and converts them into alcohol. Different varieties of grapes and strains of yeasts are used depending on the type of wine being produced.

16th century wine press

Although other fruits such as apples and berries can also be fermented, the resultant wines are normally named after the fruit from which they are produced (for example, apple wine or elderberry wine) and are generically known as fruit wine or country wine (not to be confused with the French term vin de pays). Others, such as barley wine and rice wine (i.e., sake), are made from starch-based materials and resemble beer and spirit more than wine, while ginger wine is fortified with brandy. In these cases, the use of the term "wine" is a reference to the higher alcohol content, rather than production process. The commercial use of the English word "wine" (and its equivalent in other languages) is protected by law in many jurisdictions.

Wine has a rich history dating back to around 6000 BC and is thought to have originated in areas now within the borders of Georgia and Iran. Wine first appeared in Europe at about 4500 BC in the Balkans, and was very common in ancient Greece, Thrace and Rome. Wine has also played an important role in religion throughout history. The Greek god Dionysus and the Roman equivalent Bacchus represented wine, and the drink is also used in Catholic Eucharist ceremonies and the Jewish Kiddush.

Wine boy at a symposium

Etymology

The word "wine" comes from the Proto-Germanic "*winam," an early borrowing from the Latin *vinum*, "wine" or "(grape) vine," itself derived from the Proto-Indo-European stem *win-o- (cf. Hittite: *wiyana*, Lycian: *Oino*, Ancient Greek οἶνος - *oînos*, Aeolic Greek ϝοίνος - *woinos*).

The earliest attested terms referring to wine are the Mycenaean Greek *me-tu-wo ne-wo* meaning "the month of new wine" or "festival of the new wine" and *wo-no-wa-ti-si* meaning "wine garden", written in Linear B inscriptions.

As explained in the History section below, the earliest known cultivation of the *vitis vinifera* grapevine occurred in present-day Georgia. Although no clear evidence has been found of any linguistic connection, some scholars have noted the similarities between the words for wine in the Kartvelian (e.g. Georgian *ghvino*) Semitic (*wayn*) and Indo-European languages (e.g. Russian *vino*), hinting to the possibility that this word diffused into all these language families from a common origin. Some Georgian scholars have speculated that Georgian was the origin of this word and that it entered into the Indo-European languages via Semitic.

History

Main article: History of wine

Archaeological evidence suggests that the earliest known production of wine, made by fermenting grapes, took place in sites in Georgia and Iran, from as early as 6000 BC. These locations are all within the natural area of the European grapevine *Vitis vinifera*.

The oldest known evidence of wine production in Europe is dated to 4500 BC and comes from archaeological sites in Greece. The same sites also contain the world's earliest evidence of crushed grapes. Literary references to wine are abundant in Homer (9th century BC, but possibly composed even earlier), Alkman (7th century BC), and others. In Ancient Egypt, six of 36 wine amphoras were found in the tomb of King Tutankhamun bearing the name "Kha'y", a royal chief vintner. Five of these amphoras were designated as from the King's personal estate with the sixth listed as from the estate of the royal house of Aten. Traces of wine have also been found in central Asian Xinjiang, dating from the second and first millennia BC.

Viticulture in India has a long history dating back to the time of the Indus Valley civilization when grapevines were believed to have been introduced from Persia sometime in the 5000 BC. The first known mentioning of grape-based wines was in the late 4th century BC writings of Chanakya who was the chief minister of Emperor Chandragupta Maurya. In his writings, Chanakya condemns the use of alcohol while chronicling the emperor and his court's frequent indulgence of a style of grape wine known as *Madhu*.

A 2003 report by archaeologists indicates a possibility that grapes were used together with rice to produce mixed fermented beverages in China in the early years of 7000 BC. Pottery jars from the Neolithic site of Jiahu, Henan were found to contain traces of tartaric acid and other organic compounds commonly found in wine. However, other fruits indigenous to the region, such as hawthorn, could not be ruled out. If these beverages, which seem to be the precursors of rice wine, included grapes rather than other fruits, these grapes were of any of the several dozen indigenous wild species of grape in China, rather than from *Vitis vinifera*, which were introduced into China some 6000 years later.

In medieval Europe, the Roman Catholic Church was a staunch supporter of wine since it was necessary for the celebration of Mass. Monks in France made wine for years, storing it underground in caves to age. There is an old English recipe which survived in various forms until the nineteenth century for refining white wine using Bastard—bad or tainted *bastardo* wine.

Grape varieties

Main article: List of grape varieties

Wine is usually made from one or more varieties of the European species *Vitis vinifera*, such as Pinot Noir, Chardonnay, Cabernet Sauvignon, Gamay and Merlot. When one of these varieties is used as the predominant grape (usually defined by law as a minimum of 75% or 85%), the result is a *varietal*, as opposed to a *blended*, wine. Blended wines are not necessarily considered inferior to varietal wines; some of the world's most expensive wines, from regions like Bordeaux and the Rhone Valley, are blended from different grape varieties of the same vintage.[citation needed]

Grape vineyard

Wine can also be made from other species of grape or from hybrids, created by the genetic crossing of two species. *Vitis labrusca* (of which the Concord grape is a cultivar), *Vitis aestivalis*, *Vitis rupestris*, *Vitis rotundifolia* and *Vitis riparia* are native North American grapes usually grown for consumption as fruit or for the production of grape juice, jam, or jelly, but sometimes made into wine.

Hybridization is not to be confused with the practice of grafting. Most of the world's vineyards are planted with European *V. vinifera* vines that have been grafted onto North American species rootstock. This is common practice because North American grape species are resistant to phylloxera, a root louse that eventually kills the vine. In the late 19th century, most of Europe's vineyards (only excluding some of the driest vineyards in Southern Europe) were devastated by the bug, leading to massive vine deaths and eventual replanting. Grafting is done in every wine-producing country of the world except for Argentina, the Canary Islands and Chile, which are the only ones that have not yet been exposed to the insect.

In the context of wine production, *terroir* is a concept that encompasses the varieties of grapes used, elevation and shape of the vineyard, type and chemistry of soil, climate and seasonal conditions, and the local yeast cultures. The range of possibilities here can result in great differences between wines, influencing the fermentation, finishing, and aging processes as well. Many wineries use growing and production methods that preserve or accentuate the aroma and taste influences of their unique *terroir*. However, flavor differences are not desirable for producers of mass-market table wine or other cheaper wines, where consistency is more important. Such producers will try to minimize differences in sources of grapes by using production techniques such as micro-oxygenation, tannin filtration, cross-flow filtration, thin film evaporation, and spinning cones.

Classification

Wine grapes on a vine

Main article: Classification of wine

Regulations govern the classification and sale of wine in many regions of the world. European wines tend to be classified by region (e.g. Bordeaux, Rioja and Chianti), while non-European wines are most often classified by grape (e.g. Pinot Noir and Merlot). More and more, however, market recognition of particular regions is leading to their increased prominence on non-European wine labels. Examples of non-European recognized locales include Napa Valley in California, Willamette Valley in Oregon, Columbia Valley in Washington, Barossa Valley and Hunter Valley in Australia, Central Valley in Chile, Vale dos Vinhedos in Brazil, Hawke's Bay and Marlborough in New Zealand, Okanagan Valley and Niagara Peninsula in Canada.

Some blended wine names are marketing terms, and the use of these names is governed by trademark law rather than by specific wine laws. For example, Meritage (sounds like "heritage") is generally a Bordeaux-style blend of Cabernet Sauvignon and Merlot, and may also include Cabernet Franc, Petit Verdot, and Malbec. Commercial use of the term "Meritage" is allowed only via licensing agreements with an organization called the "Meritage Association".

European classifications

France has various appellation systems based on the concept of terroir, with classifications ranging from Vin de Table ("table wine") at the bottom, through Vin de Pays and Appellation d'Origine Vin Délimité de Qualité Supérieure (AOVDQS) up to Appellation d'Origine Contrôlée (AOC) or similar, depending on the region. Portugal has something similar and, in fact, pioneered this technique back in 1756 with a royal charter which created the "Demarcated Douro Region" and regulated wine production and trade. Germany did likewise in 2002, although their system has not yet achieved the authority of those of the other countries'. Spain, Greece and Italy have classifications which are based on a dual system of region of origin and quality of product.

Moscato d'Asti, a DOCG wine

Beyond Europe

New World wine—wines from outside of the traditional wine growing regions of Europe tend to be classified by grape rather than by *terroir* or region of origin, although there have been non-official attempts to classify them by quality.

Vintages

Main article: Vintage

A "vintage wine" is one made from grapes that were all or mostly grown in a particular year, and labelled as such. Most countries allow a vintage wine to include a portion that is not from the labelled vintage. Variations in a wine's character from year to year can include subtle differences in color, palate, nose, body and development. High-quality wines can improve in flavor with age if properly stored. Consequently, it is not uncommon for wine enthusiasts and traders to save bottles of an especially good vintage wine for future consumption.

In the United States, for a wine to be vintage dated and labeled with a country of origin or American Viticultural Area (AVA) (such as "Sonoma Valley"), it must contain at least 95% of its volume from grapes harvested in that year. If a wine is not labeled with a country of origin or AVA the percentage requirement is lowered to 85%.

Vintage wines are generally bottled in a single batch so that each bottle will have a similar taste. Climate can have a big impact on the character of a wine to the extent that different vintages from the same vineyard can vary dramatically in flavor and quality. Thus, vintage wines are produced to be individually characteristic of the vintage and to serve as the flagship wines of the producer. Superior vintages, from reputable producers and regions, will often fetch much higher prices than their average vintages. Some vintage wines, like Brunellos, are only made in better-than-average years.

Non-vintage wines can be blended from more than one vintage for consistency, a process which allows wine makers to keep a reliable market image and maintain sales even in bad years. One recent study suggests that for normal drinkers, vintage year may not be as significant to perceived wine quality as currently thought, although wine connoisseurs continue to place great importance on it.

Tasting

Main article: Wine tasting

See also: Wine tasting descriptors

Judging color is the first step in tasting a wine

Wine tasting is the sensory examination and evaluation of wine. Wines are made up of chemical compounds which are similar or identical to those in fruits, vegetables, and spices. The sweetness of wine is determined by the amount of residual sugar in the wine after fermentation, relative to the acidity present in the wine. Dry wine, for example, has only a small amount of residual sugar.

Individual flavors may also be detected, due to the complex mix of organic molecules such as esters and terpenes that grape juice and wine can contain. Experienced tasters can distinguish between flavors characteristic of a specific grape and flavors that result from other factors in wine making. Typical intentional flavor elements in wine are those imparted by aging in oak casks; chocolate, vanilla, or coffee almost always come from the oak and not the grape itself.

Banana flavors (isoamyl acetate) are the product of yeast metabolism, as are spoilage aromas such as sweaty, barnyard, band-aid (4-ethylphenol and 4-ethylguaiacol), and rotten egg (hydrogen sulfide). Some varietals can also have a mineral flavor due to the presence of water-soluble salts (like limestone).

Wine aroma comes from volatile compounds in the wine that are released into the air. Vaporization of these compounds can be sped up by twirling the wine glass or serving the wine at room temperature. For red wines that are already highly aromatic, like Chinon and Beaujolais, many people prefer them chilled.

Collecting

See also: Aging of wine and Storage of wine

Outstanding vintages from the best vineyards may sell for thousands of dollars per bottle, though the broader term **fine wine** covers bottles typically retailing at over about $US 30-50. "Investment wines" are considered by some to be *Veblen goods*—that is, goods for which demand increases instead of decreases as its price rises. The most common wines purchased for investment include those from Bordeaux, Burgundy, cult wines from Europe and elsewhere, and Vintage port. Characteristics of highly collectible wines include:

Château Margaux, a First Growth from the Bordeaux region of France, is highly collectible.

1. A proven track record of holding well over time
2. A drinking window plateau (i.e., the period for maturity and approachability) that is many years long
3. A consensus amongst experts as to the quality of the wines
4. Rigorous production methods at every stage, including grape selection and appropriate barrel-aging

Investment in fine wine has attracted fraudsters who prey on their victims' ignorance of this sector of the wine market. Wine fraudsters often work by charging excessively high prices for off-vintage or lower-status wines from famous wine regions, while claiming that they are offering a sound investment unaffected by economic cycles. Like any investment, proper research is essential before investing.

Production

Main article: Winemaking

See also: List of wine-producing countries and List of wine-producing regions

Wine production by country 2006

Rank	Country (with link to wine article)	Production (tonnes)
1	▌▌ France	5,349,333
2	▌▌ Italy	4,711,665
3	Spain	3,643,666
4	United States	2,232,000
5	Argentina	1,539,600

6	Australia	1,410,483
7	China	1,400,000
8	South Africa	1,012,980
9	Chile	977,087
10	Germany	891,600

Wine production by country 2007

Rank	Country (with link to wine article)	Production (tonnes)
1	Italy	5,050,000
2	France	4,711,600
3	Spain	3,645,000
4	United States	2,300,000
5	Argentina	1,550,000
6	China	1,450,000
7	South Africa	1,050,000
8	Australia	961,972
9	Germany	891,600
10	Chile	827,746

Wine grapes grow almost exclusively between thirty and fifty degrees north or south of the equator. The world's southernmost vineyards are in the Central Otago region of New Zealand's South Island near the 45th parallel south, and the northernmost are in Flen, Sweden, just north of the 59th parallel north.

Exporting countries

Rank	Country	1000 tonnes
1	Italy*	1,793
2	France	1,462
3	Spain*	1,337
4	Australia	762
5	Chile*	472
6	United States	369
7	Germany	316
8	Argentina	302
9	Portugal	286
10	South Africa	272
World**		8,353

Rank	Country	Market share (% of value in US$)
1	France	34.9%
2	Italy	18.0%
3	Australia	9.3%
4	Spain	8.7%
5	Chile	4.3%
6	United States	3.6%
7	Germany	3.5%
8	Portugal	3.0%
9	South Africa	2.4%
10	New Zealand	1.8%

* Unofficial figure. ** May include official, semi-official or estimated data.

The UK was the world's biggest importer of wine in 2007.

Uses

Wine is a popular and important beverage that accompanies and enhances a wide range of European and Mediterranean-style cuisines, from the simple and traditional to the most sophisticated and complex. Wine is important in cuisine not just for its value as a beverage, but as a flavor agent, primarily in stocks and braising, since its acidity lends balance to rich savory or sweet dishes.

Per capita annual wine consumption: less than 1 litre.   from 1 to 7 litres.   from 7 to 15 litres.   from 15 to 30 litres.   More than 30 litres.

Red, white, and sparkling wines are the most popular, and are known as *light wines* because they are only 10–14% alcohol-content by volume. Apéritif and dessert wines contain 14–20% alcohol, and are sometimes fortified to make them richer and sweeter.

Some wine labels suggest opening the bottle and letting the wine "breathe" for a couple of hours before serving, while others recommend drinking it immediately. Decanting—the act of pouring a wine into a special container just for breathing—is a controversial subject in wine. In addition to aeration, decanting with a filter allows one to remove bitter sediments that may have formed in the wine. Sediment is more common in older bottles but younger wines usually benefit more from aeration.

During aeration, the exposure of younger wines to air often "relaxes" the flavors and makes them taste smoother and better integrated in aroma, texture, and flavor. Older wines generally *fade*, or lose their character and flavor intensity, with extended aeration. Despite these general rules, breathing does not necessarily benefit all wines. Wine should be tasted as soon as it is opened to determine how long it should be aerated, if at all.

Religious uses

See also: Kosher wine, Christianity and alcohol, and Islam and alcohol

Ancient religions

The use of wine in religious ceremonies is common to many cultures and regions. Libations often included wine, and the religious mysteries of Dionysus used wine as a sacramental entheogen to induce a mind-altering state.

Judaism

Wine is an integral part of Jewish laws and traditions. The *Kiddush* is a blessing recited over wine or grape juice to sanctify the Shabbat or a Jewish holiday. On Pesach (Passover) during the Seder, it is a Rabbinic obligation of men and women to drink four cups of wine. In the Tabernacle and in the Temple in Jerusalem, the libation of wine was part of the sacrificial service. Note that this does not mean that wine is a symbol of blood, a common misconception which contributes to the myth of the blood libel. A blessing over wine said before indulging in the drink is: *"Baruch atah Hashem* (Adonai) *elokeinu melech ha-olam, boray p'ree hagafen"*—"Praised be the Lord, our God, King of the universe, Creator of the fruit of vine."

Christianity

See also: Christianity and alcohol and Alcohol in the Bible

The bishop elevates the chalice while the deacon fans the Gifts with the ripidion.

In Christianity, wine is used in a sacred rite called the Eucharist, which originates in Gospel accounts of the Last Supper in which Jesus shared bread and wine with his disciples and commanded his followers to "do this in remembrance of me" (Gospel of Luke 22:19). Beliefs about the nature of the Eucharist vary among denominations (see Eucharistic theologies contrasted).

While most Christians consider the use of wine from the grape as essential for validity of the sacrament, many Protestants also allow (or require) unfermented, pasteurized grape juice as a substitute. Wine was used in Eucharistic rites by all Protestant groups until an alternative arose in the late 1800s. Methodist dentist and prohibitionist Thomas Bramwell Welch applied new pasteurization techniques to stop the natural fermentation process of grape juice. Some Christians who were part of the growing temperance movement pressed for a switch from wine to grape juice, and the substitution spread quickly over much of the United States and to other countries to a lesser degree. There remains an ongoing debate between some American Protestant denominations as to whether wine can and should be used for the Eucharist or allowed as an ordinary beverage.

All alcohol is strictly forbidden under Islamic law, but especially in Persia, there has been a long tradition of drinking wine.

Islam

Alcohol is largely forbidden under Islamic law. Iran and Afghanistan used to have a thriving wine industry that disappeared after the Islamic Revolution in 1979 and earlier in Afghanistan. However, people of Nuristan in Afghanistan have produced wine since ancient times and still do so. In Greater Persia, *Mei* (Persian wine) has been a central theme of poetry for more than a thousand years.

Health effects

See also: Wine and health

Red table wine

Nutritional value per 100 g (3.5 oz)	
Energy	355 kJ (85 kcal)
Carbohydrates	2.6 g
Sugars	0.6 g
Fat	0.0 g
Protein	0.1 g
Alcohol	10.6 g
10.6 g alcohol is 13%vol. 100 g wine is approximately 100 ml (3.4 fl oz.) Sugar and alcohol content can vary. Source: USDA Nutrient database [1]	

Although excessive alcohol consumption has adverse health effects, epidemiological studies have consistently demonstrated that moderate consumption of alcohol and wine is statistically associated with a decrease in death due to cardiovascular events such as heart failure. In the United States, a boom in red wine consumption was initiated in the 1990s by the TV show *60 Minutes*, and additional news reports on the *French Paradox*. The French paradox refers to the comparatively lower incidence of coronary heart disease in France despite high levels of saturated fat in the traditional French diet. Some epidemiologists suspect that this difference is due to the higher consumption of wines by the French, but the scientific evidence for this theory is limited. The average moderate wine drinker is more likely to exercise more, to be more health conscious, and to be of a higher educational and socioeconomic class, evidence that the association between moderate wine drinking and health may be related to confounding factors.

Population studies have observed a J curve association between wine consumption and the risk of heart disease. This means that heavy drinkers have an elevated risk, while moderate drinkers (at most two five-ounce servings of wine per day) have a lower risk than non-drinkers. Studies have also found that moderate consumption of other alcoholic beverages may be cardioprotective, although the association is considerably stronger for wine. Also, some studies have found increased health benefits for red wine over white wine, though other studies have found no difference. Red wine contains more polyphenols than white wine, and these are thought to be particularly protective against cardiovascular disease.

A chemical in red wine called resveratrol has been shown to have both cardioprotective and chemoprotective effects in animal studies. Low doses of resveratrol in the diet of middle-aged mice has a widespread influence on the genetic levers of aging and may confer special protection on the heart. Specifically, low doses of resveratrol mimic the effects of what is known as caloric restriction - diets with 20-30 percent fewer calories than a typical diet. Resveratrol is produced naturally by grape skins in response to fungal infection, including exposure to yeast during fermentation. As white wine has minimal contact with grape skins during this process, it generally contains lower levels of the chemical. Other beneficial compounds in wine include other polyphenols, antioxidants, and flavonoids.

To fully get the benefits of resveratrol in wines, it is recommended to sip slowly when drinking wines. Due to inactivation in the gut and liver, most of the resveratrol in imbibed red wine does not reach the blood circulation. However, when sipping slowly, absorption via the mucous membranes in the mouth can result in up to around 100 times the blood levels of resveratrol.

Red wines from the south of France and from Sardinia in Italy have been found to have the highest levels of *procyanidins*, which are compounds in grape seeds suspected to be responsible for red wine's heart benefits. Red wines from these areas have between two and four times as much procyanidins as other red wines. Procyanidins suppress the synthesis of a peptide called endothelin-1 that constricts blood vessels.

A 2007 study found that both red and white wines are effective anti-bacterial agents against strains of *Streptococcus*. Also, a report in the October 2008 issue of *Cancer Epidemiology, Biomarkers and Prevention*, posits that moderate consumption of red wine may decrease the risk of lung cancer in men.

While evidence from laboratory and epidemiological (observational) studies suggest a cardioprotective effect, no controlled studies have been completed on the effect of alcoholic drinks on the risk of developing heart disease or stroke. Excessive consumption of alcohol can cause cirrhosis of the liver and alcoholism; the American Heart Association cautions people to "consult your doctor on the benefits and risks of consuming alcohol in moderation."

Wine's effect on the brain is also under study. One study concluded that wine made from the Cabernet Sauvignon grape reduces the risk of Alzheimer's Disease. Another study concluded that among alcoholics, wine damages the hippocampus to a greater degree than other alcoholic beverages.

Sulphites are present in all wines and are formed as a natural product of the fermentation process, and many wine producers add sulfur dioxide in order to help preserve wine. Sulfur dioxide is also added to foods such as dried apricots and orange juice. The level of added sulphites varies, and some wines have been marketed with low sulphite content. Sulphites in wine can cause some people, particularly those with asthma, to have adverse reactions.

A study of women in the United Kingdom, called The Million Women Study, concluded that moderate alcohol consumption can increase the risk of certain cancers, including breast, pharynx and liver cancer. This has led the lead author of the study, Professor Valerie Beral, to assert that there is not enough evidence to conclude that any positive health effects of red wine outweigh the risk of cancer, and is quoted as saying, "It's an absolute myth that red wine is good for you." Professor Roger Corder, author of *The Red Wine Diet*, counters that two small glasses of a very tannic, procyanadin rich wine would confer a benefit, although "most supermarket wines are low procyanadin and high alcohol."

Packaging

See also: Cork (material), Closure (bottle), Alternative wine closures, Wine bottle, Box wine, and Screw cap (wine)

Most wines are sold in glass bottles and are sealed using corks (50% of production comes from Portugal). An increasing number of wine producers have been using alternative closures such as screwcaps, or synthetic plastic "corks". In addition to being less expensive, alternative closures prevent cork taint, although they have been blamed for other problems such as excessive reduction.[citation needed]

Some wines are packaged in heavy plastic bags within cardboard boxes, and are called *box wines*, or cask wine. These wines are typically accessed via a tap on the side of the box. Box wine can maintain an acceptable degree of freshness for up to a month after opening, while bottled wine will more rapidly oxidize, and is considerably degraded within a few days.

Environmental considerations of wine packaging reveal benefits and drawbacks of both bottled and box wines. Glass used to make bottles has a decent environmental reputation, as it is completely recyclable, whereas plastics as used in box wines are typically considered to be much less environmentally friendly. However, wine bottle manufacturers have been cited for Clean Air Act violations. A New York Times editorial suggested that box wine, being lighter in package weight, has a reduced carbon footprint from its distribution. Boxed wine plastics, even though possibly recyclable, can be more labor-intensive (and therefore expensive) to process than glass bottles. And while a wine box is recyclable, its plastic wine bladder most likely is not.

Storage

Main article: Storage of wine

Wine cellars, or *wine rooms* if they are above-ground, are places designed specifically for the storage and aging of wine. In an *active* wine cellar, temperature and humidity are maintained by a climate control system. *Passive* wine cellars are not climate-controlled, and so must be carefully located. Wine is a natural, perishable food product; when exposed to heat, light, vibration or fluctuations in temperature and humidity, all types of wine, including red, white, sparkling, and fortified, can spoil. When properly stored, wines can maintain their quality and in some cases improve in aroma, flavor, and complexity as they age. Some wine experts contend that the optimal temperature for aging wine is 55 °F (13 °C), others 59 °F (15 °C). Wine refrigerators offer an alternative to wine cellars. They are available in capacities ranging from small 16-bottle units to furniture pieces that can contain 400 bottles. Wine refrigerators are not ideal for aging, but rather serve to chill wine to the perfect temperature for drinking. These refrigerators keep the humidity low, usually under 50%, which is below the optimal humidity of 50% to 70%. Lower humidity levels can dry corks out over time, allowing oxygen to enter the bottle and reduce the wine's quality.

Oak wine barrels

Related professions

Name	Description
Cooper	Craftsman of wooden barrels and casks. A cooperage is a company that produces such casks.
Garagiste	An amateur wine maker, or a derogatory term used for small scale operations of recent inception, usually without pedigree and located in Bordeaux.
Négociant	A wine merchant, most specifically those who assemble the produce of smaller growers and winemakers and sells them under their own name.
Oenologist	Wine scientist or wine chemist; a student of oenology. A winemaker may be trained as oenologist, but often hires a consultant instead.
Sommelier	A restaurant specialist in charge of assembling the wine list, educating the staff about wine, and assisting customers with their wine selections.
Terroir specialist	Someone (often a consultant or academic) with special knowledge of the interplay between the environmental factors such as soil, climate and topography - also known as terroir - and wine grape quality or wine character.
Vintner, Winemaker	A wine producer; a person who makes wine.
Viticulturist	A person who specializes in the science of grapevines. Can also be someone who manages vineyard pruning, irrigation, and pest control.

See also

Main article: Outline of wine

- Acids in wine
- Aging of wine
- Beverage
- Cork
- Fruit wine
- Glossary of wine terms
- Non-grape based wine
- Oak (wine)
- Screw cap (wine)
- Spritzer
- Wine accessory
- Wine clubs
- Wine Country
- Winemaking

References

Notes

Further reading

- Foulkes, Christopher (2001). *Larousse Encyclopedia of Wine*. Larousse. ISBN 2-03-585013-4.
- Johnson, Hugh (2003). *Hugh Johnson's Wine Companion* (5th ed.). Mitchell Beazley. ISBN 978-1840007046.
- McCarthy, Ed; Mary Ewing-Mulligan, Piero Antinori (2006). *Wine for Dummies*. HarperCollins. ISBN 0-470-04579-5.
- MacNeil, Karen (2001). *The Wine Bible*. Workman. ISBN 1-56305-434-5.
- Oldman, Mark (2004). *Oldman's Guide to Outsmarting Wine*. Penguin. ISBN 978-0142004920.
- Parker, Robert (2008). *Parker's Wine Buyer's Guide*. Simon and Schuster. ISBN 978-0743271981.
- Pigott, Stuart (2004). *Planet Wine: A Grape by Grape Visual Guide to the Contemporary Wine World*. Mitchell Beazley. ISBN 978-1840007763.
- Robinson, Jancis (2006). *The Oxford Companion to Wine* (3rd ed.). Oxford: OUP. ISBN 0-19-860990-6.
- Zraly, Kevin (2006). *Windows on the World Complete Wine Course*. Sterling. ISBN 1-4027-3928-1.

External links

- *The Guardian & Observer* Guide to Wine [1]
- The wine anorak [2] by wine writer Jamie Goode

krc:Чагъыр mwl:Bino pnb:بارش

Cocktail

A **cocktail** is an alcoholic mixed drink that contains two or more ingredients — at least one of the ingredients must be a spirit.

Cocktails were originally a mixture of spirits, sugar, water, and bitters. The word has come to mean almost any mixed drink that contains alcohol. A cocktail today usually contains one or more kinds of spirit and one or more mixers, such as soda or fruit juice. Additional ingredients may be ice, sugar, honey, milk, cream, and various herbs.

History

The earliest known printed use of the word *cocktail* was in *The Farmer's Cabinet* on April 28, 1803:

> Drank a glass of cocktail—excellent for the head...Call'd at the Doct's. found Burnham—he looked very wise—drank another glass of cocktail.

A typical cocktail, served in a cocktail glass.

The earliest definition of *cocktail* was in the May 13, 1806, edition of the *Balance and Columbian Repository*, a publication in Hudson, New York, in which an answer was provided to the question, "What is a cocktail?". It replied:

> Cocktail is a stimulating liquor composed of spirits of any kind, sugar, water, and bitters—it is vulgarly called a bittered sling and is supposed to be an excellent electioneering potion, inasmuch as it renders the heart stout and bold, at the same time that it fuddles the head. It is said, also to be of great use to a Democratic candidate: because a person, having swallowed a glass of it, is ready to swallow anything else.

Flaming cocktails.

Compare the ingredients listed (spirits, sugar, water, and bitters) with the ingredients of an Old Fashioned.

The first publication of a bartenders' guide which included cocktail recipes was in 1862 — *How to Mix Drinks; or, The Bon Vivant's Companion*, by "Professor" Jerry Thomas. In addition to listings of recipes for Punches, Sours, Slings, Cobblers, Shrubs, Toddies, Flips, and a variety of other types of mixed drinks were 10 recipes for drinks referred to as "Cocktails". A key ingredient which differentiated "cocktails" from other drinks in this compendium was the use of bitters as an ingredient, although it is not used in many modern cocktail recipes.

The first "cocktail party" ever thrown was allegedly by Mrs. Julius S. Walsh Jr. of St. Louis, Missouri, in May 1917. Mrs. Walsh invited 50 guests to her home at noon on a Sunday. The party lasted an hour, until lunch was served at 1 pm. The site of this first cocktail party still stands. In 1924, the Roman Catholic Archdiocese of St. Louis bought the Walsh mansion at 4510 Lindell Boulevard, and it has served as the local archbishop's residence ever since.

During Prohibition in the United States (1920–1933), when the sale of alcoholic beverages was illegal, cocktails were still consumed illegally in establishments known as speakeasies. The quality of the alcohol available was far lower than was previously used, and bartenders generally put forth less effort in preparing the cocktails. There was a shift from whiskey to gin, which does not require aging and is thus easier to produce illicitly.

Cocktails became less popular in the late 1960s and 1970s, as other recreational drugs became common. In the 1980s cocktails again became popular, with vodka often substituted for gin in drinks such as the martini. Traditional cocktails and gin are starting to make a comeback in the 2000s.

Etymology

There are several claims about the origin of the term *cocktail*, many of which are fanciful and almost none of which are supported by documentary evidence. The word first showed up in print in 1806 in the May 13 edition of *Balance and Columbian Repository*, published in Hudson, New York: "Cocktail is a stimulating liquor composed of spirits of any kind, sugar, water, and bitters — it is vulgarly called a bittered sling and is supposed to be an excellent electioneering potion, inasmuch as it renders the heart stout and bold, at the same time that it fuddles the head."

Derivative usages

The word *cocktail* is sometimes used figuratively for a mixture of liquids or other substances. Such a use might be, for example: "120 years of industry have dosed the area's soil with a noxious cocktail of heavy metals and chemical contaminants."

A makeshift incendiary bomb consisting of a bottle of flammable liquid (usually gasoline) with a flaming rag attached is known as a "Molotov cocktail."

Combinations of antiretroviral drugs used as AIDS therapy are frequently referred to "drug cocktails" or "AIDS cocktails."

See also

- Cocktail glass
- Cocktail shaker
- Flaming beverage
- List of cocktails
- Mixed drink

External links

- Cocktails [1] at the Open Directory Project
- A History of the Cocktail [2] - slideshow by *Life magazine*

Drinking Fun

Keg stand

Keg stand is a popular drinking ritual performed using a beer keg. Its most common form involves the drinking participant grabbing onto the keg's handles as he or she is upheld into the air by others, to the effect of doing a handstand while chugging directly from the keg. A keg stand can be performed competitively (in a case of multiple kegs), or simply for noncompetitive enjoyment. Keg stands are popular among college students. An American college student interviewed by *Time Magazine* defined a keg stand as, "Two friends suspend you by your ankles over a keg, and you guzzle as much cheap beer as quickly as you can."

Canonically, onlookers will shout out the number of seconds the drinking participant drinks for before having to stop. If in a competitive setting, an agreement is commonly made beforehand about the pressure of beer coming out. The general pressure setting is for a high-pressure stream, as low pressure pours from the keg may lead to more of a variance in the amount of beer consumed in a given count.

See also

- Alcoholism
- Binge drinking

Drinking game

Drinking games are games which involve the consumption of alcoholic beverages. These games vary widely in scope and complexity, although the purpose of most is to become intoxicated as quickly as possible. Evidence of the existence of drinking games dates back to antiquity.

The rapid consumption of alcohol, key to many drinking games, worsens judgement and decreases inhibition, and may lead to alcohol poisoning. As a result, drinking games have been banned at some American universities.

Beer pong is a common physical drinking game.

History

Ancient Greece

According to Rupert Thompson of the University of Cambridge, the earliest reference to drinking games in Western literature is from Plato's Symposium *The Drinking Party*. The game was simple: fill a bowl with wine, drink it, slap it, and pass it on to the next person. Kottabos is one of the earliest known drinking games from ancient Greece, dated to the 5th to 4th centuries BC. Players would use dregs to hit targets across the room with their wine. Often, there were special prizes and penalties for one's performance in the game.

Symposium, with scene of Kottabos - fresco from the Tomb of the Diver in Paestum, 475 BC

Ancient China

Drinking games were enjoyed in ancient China, usually incorporating the use of dice or verbal exchange of riddles. During the Tang Dynasty (618-907), the Chinese used a silver canister where written lots could be drawn that designated which player had to drink and specifically how much; for example, from 1, 5, 7, or 10 measures of drink that the youngest player, or the last player to join the game, or the most talkative player, or the host, or the player with the greatest alcohol tolerance, etc. had to drink There were even drinking game referee officials, including a 'registrar of the rules' who knew all the rules to the game, a 'registrar of the horn' who tossed a silver flag down on calling out second offenses, and a 'governor' who decided one's third call of offense. These referees were used mainly for maintaining order (as drinking games often became rowdy) and for reviewing faults that could be punished with a player drinking a penalty cup. If a guest was considered a 'coward' for dropping out of the game, he could be branded as a 'deserter' and not invited back to further drinking bouts. There was another game where little puppets and dolls dressed as western foreigners with blue eyes (Iranian peoples) were set up and when one fell over, the person it pointed to had to empty his cup of wine.

Types of games

Endurance

The simplest drinking games are endurance games in which players compete to out-drink each other. Players take turns taking shots, and the last person standing is the winner. Some games have rules involving the "cascade", "fountain" or "waterfall", which encourages each player to drink constantly from their cup so long as the player before him does not stop drinking. Such games can also favor speed over quantity, in which players race to drink a case of beer the fastest.

Tolerance games are simply about seeing which player can last the longest. It can be as simple as two people matching each other drink for drink until one of the participants "passes out". Power hour and its variant, centurion, fall under this category.

Speed

Many pub or bar games involve competitive drinking for speed and not necessarily for the quantity consumed. The object of these games may not be inebriation, but may simply involve "bragging rights" or wagers of cash which benefit the fastest drinker. Examples of such drinking games are Edward Fortyhands, boat races, case races, Tour De Franzia, beer bonging, shotgunning, flip cup(a team-based speed game), and yard. The trick to speed drinking is opening the throat.

World records

The Guinness Book of Records began to list world records for speed drinking in this category in the early 1960s. These early drinking records involved drinking beer from challenging vessels such as the yard glass, which, if not correctly mastered, resulted in the user receiving a blast of beer in his or her face. The 1969 edition of the Guinness Book lists The Broom (age 20) as having consumed a 2.5 pint yard of ale in 6.5 seconds on December 17, 1964. The 1974 edition lists Jack Boyle, age 52, of Barrow-in-Furness as having consumed a 3 pint yard of ale in 10.15 seconds on May 14,

Petrosino broke a Guinness World record in Carlisle, Pennsylvania.

1971. In the mid 1970s, Guinness began to list speed records achieved using any drinking vessel. The 1977 edition dropped the earlier records established by Hill and Boyle, and listed a 2.5 pint yard record by the RAF at Upper Heyford, Oxfordshire in 5.0 seconds and a three pint yard record established at Corby Town F.C. on January 23, 1976 in 5.5 seconds". The 1977 edition listed the new world record established at the Gingerbreadman Pub by Steven Petrosino, (age 25) of New Cumberland, Pennsylvania on June 22, 1977. Petrosino drank 1 litre of beer in 1.3 seconds. Petrosino approached the challenge scientifically, and used two specially designed half-litre drinking vessels to establish this world beer record. The 1977 edition also lists Peter G. Dowdeswell of Earls Barton for drinking two pints of beer from a single vessel in 2.3 seconds on June 11, 1975 and two litres in 6.0 seconds on 7 February 1975. These records were all dropped from the Guinness book in 1991 due to concerns about litigation.

Competitive skill games

Some party and pub games focus on the doing of a particular act of skill, rather than on either the amount a participant drinks or the speed with which they do so. Notable examples include beer pong, quarters, and chandeliers. To some extent, the focus of the players on doing the act of skill, rather than simply drinking, means that these games could be played for a longer time without participants getting significantly intoxicated.

These games, however, do not allow the participants to choose how much they drink, as this is dependent on the act of skill. This means that the drinking will necessarily be distributed unevenly between players, depending on the how skilled the players are at the act that is the basis of the game.

Thinking

Thinking games rely on the players' powers of observation, recollection, logic and articulation. Such games are not difficult at the onset, but become much more challenging as the game continues as players become inebriated and their coordination and memory deteriorate.

Numerous types of thinking games exist, including 21, Pim Pom Pam, beer checkers, bizz buzz, buffalo, bullshit, tourettes, matchboxes, never have I ever, roman numerals, fuzzy duck, pennying, and zoom schwartz profigliano. Trivia games, such as Trivial Pursuit, are sometimes played as drinking games.

Physical

Several games involve a skill such as scoring a ping-pong or darts. Players must have good aim throughout the entire game, even as they become increasingly inebriated. Examples of these games include beer pong, caps, pong, beer darts and blackout.

Card and dice

Several popular drinking games involving cards are asshole, fuck the dealer, horserace, Kings, liar's poker, pyramid, bloody knuckles, Ring of Fire, ride the bus and the Flemmo.

Dice games include beer die, dudo, kinito, kranen, liar's dice, Mexico, mia, pounce!, ship, captain, and crew, tablero da Gucci, Polish Poker, and three man. Recently on the rise is the use of alcohol in games such as Dungeons and Dragons, where players must drink due to poorly rolled dice.

Kings is played with cards.

Film

Film drinking games are played while watching a movie (sometimes a TV show or a sporting event) and have a set of rules for who drinks when and how much based on on-screen events and dialogue. The rules may be the same for all players, or alternatively players may each be assigned rules related to particular characters. The rules are designed so that rarer events require larger drinks. Rule sets for such games are usually arbitrary and local, although they are sometimes published by fan clubs.

Matching the characters in the film Withnail and I has become an accepted drinking game, although the levels of consumption required for a single player are hazardous.

Music

Rock and pop music tracks can also be used as a basis for drinking games. "Roxanne" by The Police is one example.. Another example of this is the use of "The Tequila Song" by The Champs in the drinking game Vicky Tequila. One more example is the song "Thunderstruck" by ACDC in which players take a drink every time the word thunder is sung.

Sporting events

Sport related drinking games involve the participants each selecting a scenario of the game resulting their drink being downed. Examples of this include participants each picking a footballer in a game. Should this player score or sent off a drink must be taking, or extreme versions include a drink for every touch a player takes of the ball. Multiple players may also be selected.

An up-and-coming category of drinking games, athletic races involving alcohol are becoming more prevalent. An athletic contest of this kind is the beer mile, which consists of a mile run with a can of beer consumed before each of the four laps. A variant of this game is known in German speaking countries as Bierkastenlauf (beer crate running): A team of two is carrying a crate of beer along a route of several kilometers and has to consume all bottles prior to crossing the finish line. Another example is The Hurt Locker Drinking Game, in which contestants employ both speed of drinking and running.

Drinking can also be involved in variations of sports. For example, Keg Wiffleball is a drinking game based on baseball. Participants should be wary of this risks involved in this type of drinking game.

See also

- Binge drinking
- Pub Golf

References

Resources

- Benn, Charles (2002). *China's Golden Age: Everyday Life in the Tang Dynasty*. Oxford: Oxford University Press. ISBN 0-19-517665-0.
- Schafer, Edward H. (1963). *The Golden Peaches of Samarkand: A study of T'ang Exotics*. University of California Press. Berkeley and Los Angeles. 1st paperback edition: 1985. ISBN 0-520-05462-8.

External links

- Drinking Games [1] at the Open Directory Project

Funnel

A **funnel** is a pipe with a wide, often conical mouth and a narrow stem. It is used to channel liquid or fine-grained substances into containers with a small opening. Without a funnel, spillage would occur.

A typical kitchen funnel.

Funnels are usually made of stainless steel, glass, or plastic. The material used in its construction should be sturdy enough to withstand the weight of the substance being transferred, and it should not react with the substance. For this reason, stainless steel or glass are useful in transferring diesel, while plastic funnels are useful in the kitchen. Sometimes disposable paper funnels are used in cases where it would be difficult to adequately clean the funnel afterwards (for example, in adding motor oil to a car). Dropper funnels, also called dropping funnels or tap funnels, have a tap to allow the controlled release of a liquid.

The term "funnel" is sometimes used to refer to the chimney or smokestack on a steam locomotive and usually used in referring to the same on a ship. There is also a type of spider known as a funnel-web due to its habit of building its web in the shape of a funnel. The term "funnel" is even applied to other seemingly strange objects like a smoking pipe or even a humble kitchen bin.

Laboratory funnels

See Funnels (laboratory)

A Büchner funnel with a sintered glass disc

There are many different kinds of funnels that have been adapted for specialized applications in the laboratory. Filter funnels, thistle funnels (shaped like thistle flowers), and dropping funnels have stopcocks which allow the fluids to be added to a flask slowly. For solids, a powder funnel with a wide and short stem is more appropriate as it does not clog easily.

When used with filter paper, filter funnels, Buchner and Hirsch funnels can be used to remove fine particles from a liquid in a process called filtration. For more demanding applications, the filter paper in the latter two may be replaced with a sintered glass frit.

Separatory funnels are used in liquid-liquid extractions.

Construction

Glass is the material of choice for laboratory applications due to its inertness compared with metals or plastics. However, plastic funnels made of nonreactive polyethylene are used for transferring aqueous solutions. Plastic is most often used for powder funnels which do not come into contact with solvent in normal use.

In culture

The inverted funnel is a symbol of madness. It appears in many Medieval depictions of the mad. For example in Hieronymus Bosch's The Ship of Fools and The Allegory of Gluttony and Lust.

In popular culture, the Tin Woodman in L. Frank Baum's classic novel *The Wonderful Wizard of Oz* (and in most dramatizations of it) uses an inverted funnel for a hat, though that is never specifically mentioned in the story - it originated in W.W. Denslow's original illustrations for the book.

See also

- Funnelling
- Tundish, used in plumbing and continuous casting

External links

- Tundish [1]

frr:Traachter

Shotgunning

Shotgunning is a means of consuming a canned beverage, especially beer, very quickly by punching a hole in the side of the can. With this method, it is possible to easily drink a canned beverage in under 10 seconds.

Technique

To shotgun a beverage, a small hole is punched in the side of the can, close to the bottom. In order to prevent the liquid from spilling out while the cut is made, the can is held horizontally, tilted slightly, and the hole is made in the resulting air pocket. The hole can be made with any sharp object (usually a key, bottle opener, pen, knife, other sharp instrument, or possibly teeth or a thumb with enough experience). The drinker then places his or her mouth over the hole while rotating the can straight up. When the can's tab is pulled, the liquid will quickly drain through the hole into the drinker's mouth.

The Old Town Inn in Elgin, Illinois is known to be the first bar that a beer was shotgunned. As related on page 12 of Horst Veiners auto-biography "My Lush Life" published in 1936: "Then that old fool, "Irish", as we called him, stabbed his can with his bastard blade and drank from the upturned mouth the whole of the can of Krueger's finest. Karl the owner was impressed and said so. Then someone said to turn up the radio because "The Fuhrer" was about to speak."

Media

- The method of shotgunning a beer is demonstrated by John Cusack and Daphne Zuniga in the 1985 film *The Sure Thing*.
- In the 1993 film *Dazed and Confused*, teenagers are seen shotgunning beer at a party in the park.
- Film critic James Lipton once appeared on *Late Night With Conan O'Brien* and shotgunned a beer to celebrate spring-break week.
- In the 2007 comedy film *Superbad*, the characters Seth, Evan and Fogle are seen shotgunning cans of beer in a flashback.
- The 2002 mockumentary film *Fubar* features the main characters demonstrating and explaining the philosophy behind shotgunning beers.

See also

- Binge drinking
- Drinking culture
- Funneling

External links

- How to Shotgun a Beer [1] - Video by Howcast
- How to Shotgun a Beer [2] - Article on wikiHow

Never have I ever

"Never have I ever", (also known as **"I've Never..."**, **"I Never"**, or **"Ten Fingers"**,) is a popular party game that typically involves drinking. The verbal game is started with each player getting into a circle and putting up all ten fingers. Then, the first player says a simple statement starting with "Never have I ever". Anyone who has done what the first player has not must drink and put down one finger. Play then continues around the circle, and the next person makes a statement. The game is finished when any player ends up with all ten fingers down. There is an alternative form of the game in which the players drink indefinitely, and it generally ends in the early hours of the morning, when those players who haven't passed out decide that they should call it a night, though drinking in excess is not a necessary part of the game.

Games such as never have I ever "reveal interesting things about the participants and help build friendships", according to one American college student. Players often admit to things that they previously had not. As with truth or dare, the game is often sexual in nature. In some variations, the game may be incorporated into other drinking games, usually Kings.

The game has been portrayed in many television shows and films, such as *Being Erica*, *One Tree hill*, *Lost*, *The L Word*, *Family Guy*, *Big Brother*, *Frasier*, *Veronica Mars*, *Gossip Girl*, *Greek*, *Beerfest*, "ER", *Loving Annabelle*, "Degrassi: The Next Generation", and *The Boat That Rocked*.

Pennying

Pennying is a drinking game popular amongst students attending various universities throughout the United Kingdom. It is one of the International Drinking Rules, or Pub Rules. Unlike most drinking games, the rules of pennying are almost never explicitly declared to be in force; rather, by putting oneself in a social situation involving the consumption of alcohol, one is implicitly subjected to the rules should a "Pennying" situation occur. This state of affairs is most likely to be enforced at dinners known as Formal Halls where cheap wine is drunk and it is common for complete strangers to "Penny" each other. In Cambridge, pennying is especially prevalent at "formal hall swaps", or other dinner equivalent, between two dining societies- one female, one male. In most cases, sufficient wine will be provided so that there is enough to go round, and hence the aim is to get other people to drink as much as possible, or to avoid drinking oneself, due to the copious resources available. The occurrence is less common in pubs where drinks are larger and more expensive.

Rules Of Pennying

Accepted rules

Should someone manage to slip a penny into another person's drink after officially announcing pennying will take place on the night, the owner of the drink must completely consume it in one go, as fast as possible.

- The victim of the pennying is thereafter said to have been "pennied".
- The person whose drink the pennier is about to penny, has to be touching the glass or holding the glass as you cannot penny a drink with nobody around and claim for the other person to drink.
- The pennier cannot penny a glass that he or she has poured. As such, cooperation is often an essential part of the pennying process.
- A person unknowingly slipping a penny into a drink that already contains one is obliged to consume that drink as if he or she themselves had been pennied (double-pennying).
- The pennier must have a quantity of drink in his or her own glass to be eligible to penny. If someone pennies when his or her glass is empty, he or she is obliged to refill the glass and drink from it as if he or she has been pennied. The phrase employed is "an empty glass is a full glass".
- The owner of a pennied drink is allowed to keep the penny. Therefore, a "pennied" person has the small comfort of a free penny at the end of their forfeit, whereas someone guilty of "double-pennying" must forfeit both pennies to the owner of the drink.
- It is generally frowned upon, possibly even to the point of taboo, to refuse to drink a pennied beverage, or to "double-penny" intentionally a beverage with the intention of earning a free drink.
- If someone tries to penny a glass, but misses, he or she must down their own drink.

- In Australia, the official currency denomination used for pennying is either the five cent (5c) coin or the ten cent (10c) coin, depending which university one considers. Pennying in Australia is known more widely as coining, or 'God Save the Queen', where one must save the 'Queen' (that is, the image of the queen imprinted on the coin) from drowning.
- Paper money is invalid for the purposes of pennying. (See 'History of Pennying' below; as paper floats, the drink poses no danger to the Sovereign.)
- If the person who has been pennied catches the coin between his teeth, then the pennier must down his own drink/pint.

Variations and additional rules

Whether you follow these rules will likely depend on social pressure; bear in mind that there is no standard set of rules that you are obligated to follow. Where guests from one college are dining at another's formal hall, the rules followed by the hosts tend to apply. Dubious sources of authority are often cited, for example, at Cambridge, quite often the Presidents of college "Dining Societies" are said to arbitrate on the rules.

- At University College, Durham University, pennying is instead known as corking - unsurprisingly involving the use of corks rather than pennies. Special status is granted to Champagne corks pretty much universally, and black corks less so. The exact rules of these variant corks differ from social group to social group and from time-to-time.
- Much discussion exists over rules regarding pennying an empty glass. In some places this is frowned upon, but in many Durham and Cambridge Colleges the "Empty glass is a full glass rule" is often enforced. In these situations, if a diner has an empty glass pennied, the diner must fill it up and down it. This leads to certain elements of trickery, for example, if a glass has a small amount of wine in it, a potential pennier will double penny the near-empty glass, finish it, and then penny the glass, forcing the glass's owner to down a full glass.
- In some places, a drink may only be pennied once the owner has drunk from it, unless the owner poured his/her own beverage (accepting the drink). In Cambridge, however, such a rule tends not to exist.
- Suitably liquid foods may be used in place of drinks: soup and yogurt are two prime targets. The victim must finish the pennied item of food in one go and without the use of cutlery.
- Similarly, a dessert may be pennied, the objective being to consume it hands free. However, this, in some Cambridge Colleges, must be done with a 5p piece. Here, the victim has been "silvered", and must thus consume their dessert without silver ware. A 19 year old student was once expelled from Cambridge university after maliciously 'silvering' Steven Hawkings' dessert.
- Some would maintain - particularly in Durham Colleges - that one should not place one's hand over a glass or bottle ('guarding') in order to avoid its being pennied.
- If there are no pennies to hand (or if pennies have been banned due to their damaging effect on dishwashers), special powers may be invoked by which honorary penny status is conveyed upon a

seemingly mundane object such as a fork, spoon or Smartie. To convey such a status one must place the item in the target beverage and declare it to be "The Knife of Strife", "The Spoon of Doom", or some such other rhyming title.

- In some places, Double-penniers are required, in addition to consuming the double-pennied drink, to replace the drink owner's drink with one equivalent in genre and volume to the pennied beverage, or alternatively of the owner's choosing (of a similar price). This acts as an effective deterrent to those who would intentionally double-penny a drink with the goal of winning a free one. This is usually not a problem at Oxford and Cambridge formal halls, due to the large amounts of wine that tends to be available.
- At University College, Durham (and possibly other colleges, albeit with pennies), however, a double-corking is both allowed and results in the "cork-ee" having to down their drink immediately.
- Coins not featuring the reigning Sovereign (foreign coins and those featuring deceased monarchs) do not incur the "pennying" forfeit as their submerged nature poses no metonymical danger to the Sovereign (see History Of Pennying below). Test cases involving abdicated monarchs are not known to have arisen while one was still alive (the only example in British history being Edward VIII), though theoretically a Pennied person would owe no allegiance to someone not of the direct line of succession of the British Royal Family.
- In most Oxbridge colleges, once an individual has pennied a fellow diner they are then immune from being pennied by the initial penny-ee until the penny-ee has pennied another diner. Should the initial penny-ee proceed to penny the initial penner without the prior pennying of a separate individual then this shall be declared to be a back-pennying and thus invalid. This rule is intended to disestablish cliques or vendettas which may form and promote social interaction.
- In most Cambridge colleges, anyone holding his or her glass above the surface of the table is immune from being pennied at that moment.
- In most Oxford colleges, a drink can only be pennied if the owner of the drink is touching or holding the glass. If an individual pennies a glass that the owner is not touching, then the pennier must down his or her own drink.
- A variation on the pennying tradition is Shoeing - if there is a spillage resulting from an unsuccessful pennying attempt, or any another unsocial/drunken act, the senior member of the table is obliged to remove his shoe. It is presented as a receptacle for the remains of the unpennied wine, which must then be drunk from the shoe by the pennying miscreant. This is used during Boat Club crew-dates at Oriel College, Oxford.
- At the Royal Veterinary College, University of London, you may be required to funnel your drink instead of just downing it, however this is subject to appropriate chanting by surrounding drinkers.
- Pennying has even managed to adapt to the narrow-necked alcopop bottles - these are no longer safe from pennies folded in a vice, which are thus slim enough in profile to be dropped into the bottles through their openings. The pennies are called engineer's pennies and are often created by undergraduate engineers.

- Members of the Trinity Hall Guards must not penny other member Guards. Failure to comply will result in communal punishment. In the past this usually constitutes the requirement of guilty Guard to 'down' the remnants of his bottle of wine.
- At St Andrews University, particularly among the students of the United College, the game is referred to as 'Save the Queen', and a song is sung once the act of pennying has been carried out. It is considered bad form for a bejant to penny an older year. The concept involves the fact that the queens head is submerged in the drink and thus she is drowning - this requires the immediate action of consuming the whole drink quickly in order to ' save the queen '.
- In some schools and colleges, the person who has been pennied must down their drink before a chant, sung by those around them, has finished. Such a chant generally lasts around 15 seconds.

Alternatives to Pennying

If the act of Pennying with a penny has been banned then there are accepted alternatives which can be used instead. These include Smarties, Lovehearts, M&Ms, or a bottle cap folded in half. Note that Pennying accompanies the International Drinking Rules observed in some social circles.

Corking

At University College, Durham (also known as 'Castle', due to its being based in Durham Castle as the oldest of the Durham colleges), corking is enforced in Formal Hall. This makes use of traditional cork corks, metal wine bottle caps and champagne corks. The standard rules require that the glass to be corked is not held at the time. If a drink is corked, the owner must down the wine the next time he touches the glass. However if another corker adds a second cork (double corking) the drink must be downed immediately. Some debate ensues between social groups as to whether one corker may cork with more than one cork. A person may call 'last glass' if they have already had three glasses or if it is the last of their wine, but this must be heard by at least four people immediately after being poured. It is illegal to cork a 'last glass', and some group maintain that the corker must down their own glass if accidentally corking a last glass. The 'four cork' rule is generally played in which four corks counteract the last glass rule, requiring the drink to be downed. Champagne corks hold a special status, requiring the current glass, and a subsequent glass, to be downed immediately. Some members also consider a champagne cork to be worth three ordinary corks. Glasses should be kept over half full at all times- a corked glass containing less than this is requires the contents, plus a subsequent glass, to be downed. If the glass is empty a full glass must be downed, and some members play that another after this must also be drunk immediately. In the Undercroft Bar of the college corking is not played, and instead pennying is employed. In addition to standard rules, if the person pennied can correctly predict the date on the penny they are not obliged to drink, but the pennyer must drink their own drink instead.

Variations between universities

The University of Bath Snowsports Club, and other Sporting and Social groups affiliated with the University of Bath, engage in "Golf Balling". Essentially, a golf ball is dropped into the beverage. The beverage must must be consumed whilst spectators sing "We Like To Drink With Barney, 'cos Barney is our mate, he lives for fornication, and likes to masturbate. Get it down, you zulu warrior, get it down you zulu CHIEF CHIEF CHIEF CHIEF (until they finish)", replacing Barney with the drinker's name. When golf balls have not been available, other items such as water-proof cameras have been known to be used. The same rules apply to golf balling (or similar alternatives) as to pennying. The most important variation of the Bath Snow Sports game is that any beverage is in play as long as a person has christened it (drunk from it) and, importantly, that it is arms reach of that person. The person does not have to be holding the beverage for them to be 'golf balled'

The Oxford and the Cambridge rules vary. In Oxford, one must have the glass in one's hand for it to be eligible for pennying, the only exception being at dinners in the Great Hall of Christ Church, Oxford where such a condition is not required for a pennying to be valid. If a glass on the table is pennied, the pennier must forthwith down the beverage, and buy the intended pennyee a replacement. In Cambridge there is no such rule and pennying may occur at any time, or sometimes the exact opposite rule is played.

The University of Durham has a variety of rules varying from college to college. The vast majority of colleges require penny-ies to be touching their glass. In Hatfield College, Durham rules are used that are similar to those stated above for Oxford, except that two pence coins are used instead of pennies, and pennying the water jug is generally seen as fair game, although liable to incur a "sconce" (or fine) from the JCR Senior Man. A further example would be University College, Durham whose members utilise corks in place of pennies. This leads to corks being a valuable commodity amongst castle undergraduates, and rules dictating who owns the cork in someone's drink are complicated and vary between friendship groups. Some also play rules that differentiate between different types of cork (for example, a champagne cork might result in two glasses being downed). Castlemen also play differently to most other Durham colleges in that they only can only 'cork' when their victim's glass is on the table (but in the case of liquid food, it must be held, to show possession). At Grey College, pennying at Formals was banned by the Master (Prof. Martyn Chamberlain) in 2003. At Trevelyan College, some students have taken to bending 2p coins so they may fit down the neck of a wine bottle, which then must be downed. Double pennying results in the second pennier only having to down their drink, and not the penny-ie. The rules of pennying are generally considered more liberal in the hill colleges, and in some colleges, pennying occurs in the bar at any time.

The University of Bristol rules state that for a glass to be "in play" some of the contents must have been imbibed by the owner, and the owner must be at the table. Shielding of glasses is therefore very common and is not frowned upon. Any coins bearing the monarch's face may be used, although coppers tend to be the most popular. Double Pennying is not regarded as an offence on the person adding the second (or further) coin but rather a shameful act on the part of the person who has been pennied for not finishing their drink with alacrity.

At St Andrews the game is played in all colleges and referred to as 'save the queen.' The only rules being that a bejant may not penny anybody apart from a fellow bejant. There is wide variation on the specifics across the halls/societies.

Pennying has been explicitly banned from Pembroke College, St. Anne's College and Brasenose College, Oxford, as well as Jesus College and Magdalene College, Cambridge. Brasenose's code of conduct refers to the illicit activity as "the practice of dropping a coin in a cup to coerce someone to consume the contents." Student Newspapers reported that the St Anne's College authorities and the Junior Common Room had come into serious conflict when the Freshers of 2006 were informed that pennying remained 'a forbidden pleasure' in one of their guides to the college.

At Cardiff University, those within the student media societies (particularly Xpress Radio) drop badges into drinks bearing other radio station logos. However, only one badge is "in play" at any one time.

The Royal Veterinary College in London follows standard pennying rules, however in foreign countries the use of the smallest coin is acceptable even though it lacks the queen. You may also be required to funnel your drink instead of just downing it but this is subject to appropriate chanting from the surrounding drinkers.

History of Pennying

The oft-quoted reason given for the need to "drink up" is that the Sovereign (depicted on the obverse or "heads" side of the submerged penny) is in danger of drowning and must be rescued immediately. Cries of "God Save the Queen!" may be heard, uttered immediately prior to the consumption of the beverage. No canonical text outlines the custom of pennying, hence the great variations in its practised rules. Despite there being no evidence that this practice goes back more than a few decades, apocryphal tales and oral tradition among some within the University of Cambridge would attribute its origin to the time of the reign of Henry VIII.

While the historicity of this account of the origin of Pennying is almost as doubtful as the validity of its posing actual mortal danger to the Sovereign, Pennying has certainly lasted long enough to become a credible tradition within Oxford, Cambridge and a few other places (such as the University of St Andrews) elsewhere in the United Kingdom.

This practice is similar but probably unrelated to the (almost certainly older) practice of sconcing at Oxford.

References

- Anger after college bans pennying News Article, Pg 7, "The Cherwell", October 4, 2006
- A penny for your thoughts Editorial, "The Oxford Student", October 4, 2006
- ^ http://www.bbc.co.uk/dna/getwriting/A882722
- "Student handbook" [1]. Clare College, Cambridge. 2007. Retrieved 2008-11-08.
- Whitney, Anna (2001-10-30). "Cambridge college dean tells students to sober up" [2]. London: *The Independent*. Retrieved 2008-11-08.
- "A penny for your thoughts" [3]. *The Oxford Student*. 2006-10-04. Retrieved 2008-12-16.
- "Univ Freshers' handbook" [4]. University College, Oxford JCR. Retrieved 2008-12-16.
- "Downing College MCR: Glossary" [5]. Downing College, Cambridge MCR. 2008-03-19. Retrieved 2008-12-16.
- Chrisafis, Angelique (2001-11-06). "Behaving rather badly" [6]. London: *The Guardian*. Retrieved 2008-12-16.
- Rudd, Alfred (2007-01-26). "Formal" [7]. *Varsity*. Retrieved 1008-12-16. "Pennying Stephen Hawking, always rather to be frowned upon, still makes a funny story"
- "Blue Book" [8]. Brasenose College, Oxford. 2006. Retrieved 2008-12-16.
- "JCR Handbook" [9]. St Anne's College, Oxford. 2008. Retrieved 2008-12-16. Wikipedia:Link rot
- "Meal Information" [10]. Trinity Hall, Cambridge. Retrieved 2008-12-16.
- Lightfoot, Liz (2001-10-30). "Dean reads riot act over 'drunken, naked girls'" [11]. London: *The Telegraph*. Retrieved 2008-12-16.
- Harris, Sarah. "Sober up girls, Dean warns" [12]. *The Daily Mail*. Retrieved 2008-12-16.
- Carlson, Annika (2007-04-09). "Brits get Boozed" [13]. *The Nation*. Retrieved 2008-12-16.
- "Cambridge porters given hepatitis jabs to protect against bingeing students" [14]. *The Daily Mail*. 2007-03-06. Retrieved 2008-12-16.
- "Boozy students are a sick joke for Porters" [15]. *Cambridge News*. 2007-03-06. Retrieved 2008-12-16.
- Smith, Ben. "Glossary" [16]. Van Mildert College, Durham JCR. Retrieved 2008-12-16.

Beer pong

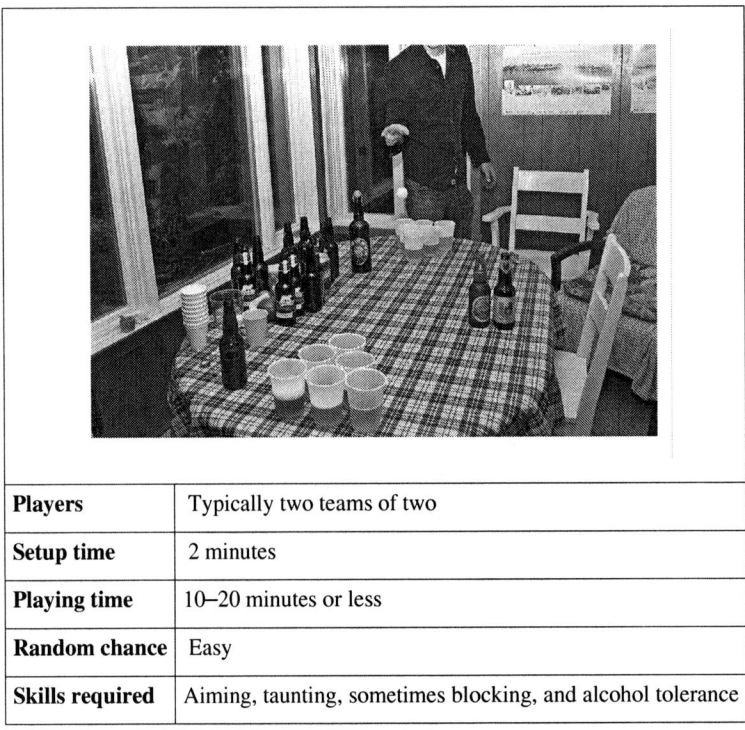

Players	Typically two teams of two
Setup time	2 minutes
Playing time	10–20 minutes or less
Random chance	Easy
Skills required	Aiming, taunting, sometimes blocking, and alcohol tolerance

Beer Pong, also known as Beirut, is a drinking game in which players throw a ping-pong ball across a table with the intent of landing the ball in a cup of beer/water on the other end. The game typically consists of two two-to-four-player teams and multiple cups set up on each side set up in triangle formation. There are no official rules, so rules may vary widely, though usually there are six or ten plastic cups arranged in a triangle on each side.

The order of play varies—both players on one team shoot followed by both players on the other team, or players on opposite teams can alternate back and forth.

Venues

Today, beer pong is played at parties, North American colleges and universities and elsewhere, such as tailgating or other sporting events. The game is also played by high school students, despite the fact that supplying alcohol to underage persons is illegal in the U.S.

Although the preceding guidelines are common, the rules may be subject to a wide variety of modifications and additions that often vary based on the area of the country, the state, or even the house in which a particular game of beer pong is played. For example a rule accepted in some households would be that at the start of a game you can win by scoring from throwing a behind the back shot, while others allow a behind the back shot worth only one cup if you retrieve your own rebound without it hitting the ground.

Origin and name

The game evolved from the original beer pong played with paddles which is generally regarded to have had its origins within the fraternities of Dartmouth College in the 1950s and '60s, where it has since become part of the social culture of the campus. The original version resembled an actual ping pong game with a net and one or more cups of beer on each side of the table. Eventually, a version without paddles was created, and later the names *Beer Pong* and *Beirut* were adopted in some areas of the USA sometime in the 1980s.

The names *Beirut* and *Beer Pong* are generally synonyms for the version without paddles, but in some places *Beer Pong* refers to the version with paddles, and *Beirut* to the version without. However, according to a CollegeHumor survey, *beer pong* is a more common term than *Beirut* for the paddle-less game. The origin of the name "Beirut" is disputed. A 2004 op-ed article in the *Daily Princetonian,* the student newspaper at Princeton University, suggested that the name was coined at Bucknell University or Lehigh University around the time of the Lebanese Civil War, Beirut being the capital of Lebanon and scene of much fighting. Others attribute the origin of *Beirut* to Lehigh, where fraternities allegedly started playing after all beer pong paddles were broken. Some students at Lafayette College, rivals of Lehigh, insist modern, paddle-less beer pong was invented at their school, but *The Lafayette,* the college's student newspaper, says there is no proof to back up the assertion.

Setup

Teams

Beer pong is usually played with two teams of two players each, though it can be played with two teams of other numbers of players. Each team begins the game standing at either end of the table behind their rack of cups.

Playing field

Although the game is typically played on either a ping pong table or a folding banquet table, enthusiasts may create a personalized table for use by friends and visitors. In general, this will be a plywood board cut to proper size, sometimes painted with sports, school, or fraternity symbols and given a liquid-proof coating. Some companies sell tables, and there are companies making portable or inflatable tables. The game can be played on any flat surface, most typically a dining table.

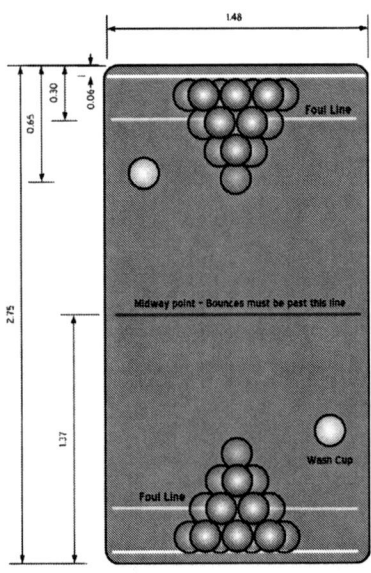

This diagram illustrates a standard set up for a game of Beirut, with either 6 or 10 cups being used.

Equipment

The most common cups used are 16 ounce disposable plastic cups (such as red Solo cups) with ridge-lines which can be used precisely to measure the amount of beer to be poured into the cup. On each side of the table, teams assemble equilateral triangles, with a convergence point focusing on the other team. Games typically use either six, ten, or twelve cups. Each team usually has a separate cup of water as well, used to rinse off the ball.

38 mm or 40 mm table tennis (ping pong) balls are typically used for game play.

Alcohol

An inexpensive pale lager or light beer of 3.2–5% ABV is sometimes preferred because of the large quantities of beer which may be consumed during the course of several games. For non-drinkers, the game may be played without beer, as is done at Utah State University, where alcohol is not allowed on campus—root beer is used instead. The game may also be played with water instead of beer, or with cups full of water that players do not drink from, instead using another cup of beer or alcohol. Water pong has been banned at some freshman Dartmouth dorms due to a possibility of water intoxication.

Game play

There are very few universal or "official" rules. Typically, players abide by a uniform set of "house rules", which are often consistent within one university or region of the country (e.g., "Ivy League rules" or "West Coast rules"), or may vary on a "house-by-house" basis. Number of cups, bouncing, amount of alcohol, the distance shots must be taken from, et cetera, may all vary.

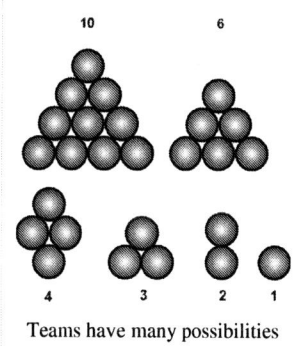

Teams have many possibilities for reracks.

In some house rules, players must immediately drink any cup that has been hit. Failure to do so incurs a penalty, such as drinking more beer or losing the game. Some rule sets allow for "*re-racking*" (also known as "*rearranging*", "*consolidation*", and other names), which is a rearrangement of a team's remaining cups after some have been removed. The formations, number of cups, when to rearrange and so on depend on the rule set. For example, a team with three remaining cups may ask the other team to "re-rack" their multiple targets into a single triangle formation.

Some other house rules allow swatting the ball away if it bounces and blowing the ball out of the cup if the ball spins around the inner rim. Other rules state that if a team makes both shots in a round, they may shoot again, sometimes called a "repo" or "rollback". In World Series of Beer Pong rules only one repo/rollback is allowed and is a single ball. If this ball is also made the three consecutive shots are referred to as a "splash-trick".

After shooting, teams may dunk the ping pong balls into cups of water in order to wash off the balls. However, research showed that the wash cups still hold bacteria, such as *E. coli*.

Shot techniques

There are three key ways to shoot in beer pong: the arc, the fastball (or "laser"), and the bounce shot. The most common throwing technique is the "arc" shot, where one grasps the ping pong ball with the tips of the thumb and forefinger, holds the arm at an angle with the ball upwards, then throw by using gentle elbow motion, holding the upper arm parallel with the table.

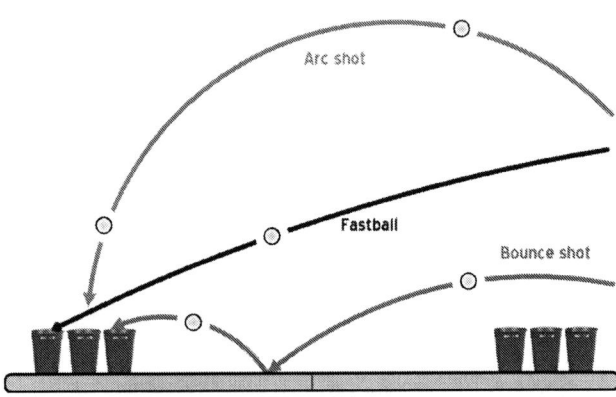

The typical path for the different kinds of shots.

Some players throw "fastball" style, which uses more of a hard chopping motion to send the ball in a more direct line to the intended target cup. Also, a fastball shot may be favorable if house rules dictate a cup that is knocked over is taken off the table, in which case a fastball can eliminate multiple cups if thrown hard enough.

A "bounce" shot is performed by bouncing the ball toward the cups. Since (depending on house rules) the other team may have the opportunity to swat away a bounced ball, a bounce may be worth more than one cup. In some rule sets, bouncing is not allowed; in others, it is required.

Winning the game

If the opposing team makes the last cup, the other loses unless they can make either all remaining cups or simply one cup, depending on "house rules"—this is called a rebuttal or redemption. In some rule sets, if the opposing team hits the last cup with both of their balls, no redemption is given to the losing team.

A shutout rule is a house rule usually stated before a game or during the game in the midst of a shutout. If the shutout does occur the losing team must do whatever the two teams decided on, such as going streaking or drinking a large quantity of beer.

Health effects

This game may have several health issues associated with it. Beer pong, as with any activity involving alcohol, may cause players to become intoxicated or even drunk enough to get alcohol poisoning. Also, the supposed cleaning effects of the water "dunk" cup may be offset by bacteria in the cups.

Some writers have mentioned beer pong as contributing to "out of control" college drinking.

In early 2009, news sources claimed a recent study by the U.S. Centers for Disease Control and Prevention (CDC) stated that beer pong was contributing to the spread of herpes, mononucleosis, and other diseases through shared cups. The CDC quickly responded as the CDC had not done such research, however the U.S. National Institutes of Health (NIH) does suggest avoiding the sharing of eating utensils to prevent the transmission of certain contagious viruses such as herpes.

Legal restrictions

Some municipalities and states have attempted to ban beer pong, either from bars or in general, due to the belief that it encourages binge drinking (see Health Effects above). In Oxford, Ohio, where Miami University is located, the city council tried to ban the game from being played outdoors, and in Arlington, Virginia and Champaign-Urbana, Illinois bar owners were told to stop allowing the game to be played in their establishments. In the fall of 2007, Georgetown University officially banned all beer pong paraphernalia, such as custom-built tables and the possession of many ping-pong balls.

Time magazine ran an article on July 31, 2008 called "The War Against Beer Pong", noting legal restrictions and bans on the game in college and elsewhere.

Former Steeler and Pennsylvania Governor candidate Lynn Swann plays beer pong with tailgaters before a football game.

Tournaments and leagues

Beer pong tournaments are held in the United States at the local, regional, and national levels.

The World Series of Beer Pong (WSOBP), hosted by bpong.com, is the largest beer pong tournament in the world. WSOBP IV, held in January 2009 at the Flamingo Hotel and Casino in Las Vegas, Nevada, had a $50,000 grand prize and attracted over 800 participants from the US and Canada. WSOBP V, held in January 2010, attracted over 1,000 participants, and attracted teams from Ireland, Scotland, Germany and Japan, each of which voiced their aspirations to further the sport in their home countries. The World Beer Pong Tour has stops in various cities and cash prizes as well. Myles Marshall and Travis Erbs are the reigning beer pong champions of the world.

The National Beer Pong Showdown, hosted by Beer Pong Inc. is the first and only beer pong tournament hosted on a cruise ship. Currently, you must win a regional tournament for free entry into the national tournament. National tournaments are hosted annually on a Baja, Mexico cruise.

A more common organization of beer pong games are leagues which operate on a local or regional level. Ordinarily, a group of pong enthusiasts will create teams (partnerships) and play weekly against each other. Sometimes, the leagues have websites, rankings and statistics, while others have been started by college students with the goal of intramural competition such as at University of California, Santa Barbara with the "Isla Vista Beer Pong League", and at New York University.

Beer pong in the media

The Wall Street Journal, *Time* and other media outlets have reported on the increase in businesses selling beer pong paraphernalia, such as tables, mats, cups, or clothes. *Last Cup: Road to the World Series of Beer Pong* is a documentary which follows some competitive players as they prepare for the WSOBP II and ultimately compete against one another for the $20,000 grand prize. This documentary, directed by Dan Lindsay, premiered at the CineVegas film festival on June 13, 2008. WSOBP V attracted further media attention, with writers from *Maxim* magazine and *ESPN The Magazine* attending, and it was featured on *The Jay Leno Show* on January 8, 2010, and also on G4's *Attack of the Show!* on January 11, 2010.

The Associated Press cited the game and other drinking games as a factor in deaths of college students.

Time magazine recently had an article on the popularity of beer pong and posted a video on their website. In both, players claimed beer pong was a sport, rather than a game—similar to billiards and darts.

Rick Reilly wrote an entire column about The World Series of Beer Pong IV for *ESPN The Magazine*.

The game has been a recurring segment on *Late Night with Jimmy Fallon*, with host Fallon playing against celebrity guests such as Betty White, Serena Williams, Anna Kournikova, Charlize Theron and Jessica Alba.

The Colbert Report featured a segment on the CDC study hoax.

In *Road Trip: Beer Pong*, a sequel to 2000 comedy *Road Trip*, featured the game prominently. Agnes Scott College, where most of the movie was filmed, did not want to be listed in the credits after complaints from students.

Episode 2 ("Hazed and Confused") of the show *Greek* features a game of beer pong between two frat houses.[citation needed]

In the movie *Beerfest*, they had the original version of beer pong with paddles in it . Also they had the non paddle version calling it beirut.[citation needed]

Publishing

On August 29, 2009, Chronicle Books published *The Book of Beer Pong*, a 200 page fully illustrated guide to the game.

Bud pong

Bud pong was the branded version of beer pong that brewer Anheuser-Busch said involved the drinking of water, not Budweiser or any other beer. In the summer of 2005, the company began marketing "bud pong" kits to its distributors. Francine I. Katz, vice president for communications and consumer affairs, was reported in *The New York Times* as saying that bud pong was not intended for underage drinkers because promotions were held in bars, not on campuses. And it did not promote binge drinking, she said, because official rules call for water to be used, not beer.

The New York Times quoted a bartender at a club near Clemson University as saying she had worked at several bud pong events and had "never seen anyone playing with water. It's always beer. It's just like any other beer pong."

Some expressed incredulity at Anheuser-Busch's public statements. Henry Wechsler, director of the College Alcohol Study at the Harvard School of Public Health, said: "Why would alcohol companies promote games that involve drinking water? It's preposterous," while advertising news site Adjab opined that "someone playing bud pong with water is about as likely as a teenage kid using the rolling paper he bought at the convenience store to smoke tobacco."

Video games

In July 2008, JV Games Inc. released a downloadable video game for the Wii console called *Frat Party Games: Beer Pong*. After much outrage by parent and university groups, the game was renamed *Frat Party Games: Pong Toss* and all references to alcohol were removed.

External links

- Beer pong [1] at the Open Directory Project

Beerdarts

Beerdarts is a drinking game involving aluminum beer cans and metal darts. Although many variations exist, the basic idea is to throw a dart at your opponent's can that has been placed on the ground at their feet. If said dart makes contact with a beer can various actions take place as detailed in the rules.

Rules

1. All players must be seated or in a squatting stance with at least one can of opened beer directly in front of them.
2. There must be at least two players.
3. If a dart grazes your can but does not puncture it, you must have a sip of beer.
4. If a dart punctures your can you must drink beer to at least the hole (this version 3 holes and you slam the remainder and lose), alternate rules state you must shotgun the beer.
5. Alternate rule: If a dart punctures the top of your can you must shotgun the beer.
6. If a can is tipped over but not punctured,you also must have a sip of beer
7. If a body part is punctured, the thrower must drink.
8. A beer (sidearm) may be present in each player's hands for sipping between throws.

Variations

Classic

> Two players, one can each, with or without a mat or B-Team.

Party beerdarts

> Many players seated in a circle, one can each, with or without a B-Team. In large groups, four or more, it is often established that shooting at a direct neighbor is prohibited, at least at first.

Double beerdarts

> Same rules as Classic beerdarts except two cans are stacked on top of each other. If the bottom can is punctured, the top can must be completely consumed before the bottom can is consumed down to the puncture.

Team beerdarts

> Four or more players, all using mats, one side forms a team to play against the other side.

Local Variation(WA State)

> Played similar to beer pong, this variation has two teams (or individual players) standing 15 feet apart or more (depending on the desired challenge of the players) with cans laid on their sides in a T (two cans) or H (five cans) formation. Teams then take turns throwing three darts at the cans.

The team receiving throws at their cans must finish the punctured can(s) before they can throw. This is usually done as fast as possible, though some parties prefer a more relaxed, multiple drink approach.

Official websites

- http://www.beerdarts.com [1]
- http://www.beerdarts.ca [2]
- http://beerdarts.org [3]
- http://groups.myspace.com/beerdarts [4]

Kings (card game)

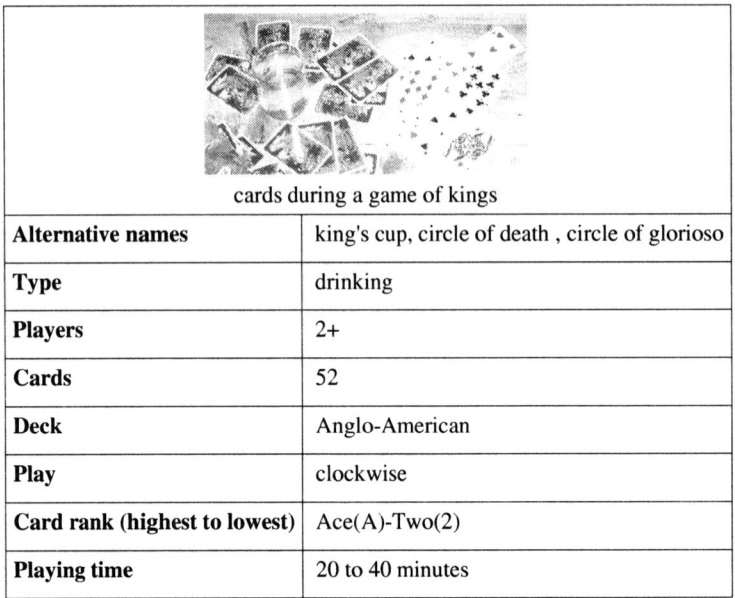

cards during a game of kings

Alternative names	king's cup, circle of death , circle of glorioso
Type	drinking
Players	2+
Cards	52
Deck	Anglo-American
Play	clockwise
Card rank (highest to lowest)	Ace(A)-Two(2)
Playing time	20 to 40 minutes

Kings (also known as **King's Cup Ring of Fire Circle of Death Rhombus of Nosferatu**, **Shanty of McGinty**, **Sociables** and **The King's Game**) is a drinking game that is played using cards. It is common among university students in Canada, New Zealand, Australia, the United States, the United Kingdom and Ireland. Players must drink and dispense drinks based on cards drawn, and kings can also be mixed with other drinking games. Each card has a rule that is pre determined before the game starts. Many houses have their own variation of rules. The game has been criticized for its contribution to binge drinking.

Rules and Setup

Equipment

- 1 deck of playing cards
- 2 or more players
- Alcoholic beverages, typically wine, beer or mixed spirits
- King's Cup (can be removed upon variation of the game)

Setup and Common Rules

In this game, players do certain actions that are associated with each card. Like many other drinking games, kings is played with different "house rules" throughout the United States and Canada. Sometimes, rules on the cards "reveal interesting things about the participants".

Usually, cards are shuffled and dealt into a circle around either an empty cup or a full can of beer (or shot/cup of spirits or wine). Each player takes turn drawing cards, and the players must participate in the instructions corresponding to the drawn card.

This game is highly open ended and all of the cards can signify any mini game, the rules and the card assignments are normally confirmed at the start of the game. Once again, depending on house rules, the game either ends when all cards have been chosen, or when the king's cup has been consumed; or when the cards are placed on top of the king's cup the game is over when the cards fall off, the one that knocked them off must consume the king's cup.

Common Card Assignments

The following is a list of the most common card assignments. They can be varied at the will of the players before the game commences.

Card Drawn	Title	Instruction
Ace	"Waterfall"	To "water fall" each player starts drinking their beverage, depending on the direction of the game (whether you are picking cards clockwise or counter clockwise). No player can stop drinking until the player before them has stopped. Vessels do not have to be fully consumed. The exception is the player who drew the ace, who may stop whenever they please. Waterfall is only recommended with beer and the like. For higher % drinks use the "Social" rule. See Variations below.
2	"You"	The player who drew the card assigns someone to drink.
3	"Me"	The player who drew the card drinks.
4	"Floor"	Everyone must touch the floor. The last player to do so must drink.
5	"Guys"	All participating men drink.
6	"Chicks"	All participating women drink.
7	"Heaven"	All players must point upwards, the last player to do so must drink.
8	"Mate / Crazy 8"	The player who drew the "8" chooses another player as a partner and both players must drink. A common variation of this rule is that from this point in the game, the player who has been picked as the "mate" must drink whenever the player who drew the "8" drinks. This is only recommended for larger groups. Crazy 8 - 8's are wild. They can be any card of the player's choosing.
9	"Rhyme"	The player who drew the 9 says a phrase, then the players go around in the circle saying phrases that rhyme with the original. No phrase may be said twice, the first player who can not come up with a phrase, or says a phrase that doesn't rhyme must drink.

10	"Categories"	The player who drew the 10 picks a category such as "sports teams" or "bands from the '90s," the players then go around in the circle saying items from that category, the first player who can not think of an item or says something not in the category (or if all items have been exhausted) must drink.
Jack	"Never have I ever"	All players hold up three fingers (five in larger groups). The player who drew the Jack says something he has never done in his life, beginning with the phrase "never have I ever" (eg. Never have I ever been to Asia). Anybody who has done what the player says must lower one finger. Play continues clockwise until one person is out of fingers, and drinks.
Queen	"Questions"	The player who drew the Queen keeps it until some one answers any question asked. The player who answers must drink or, depending on the house rules, all players must go around the circle asking questions (some variations require that the question be contextually sensible) or the player with whom the asker made eye contact with must ask a question to another player (in some circles asking to the same person loses the game). No question may be said twice (or repackaged in some versions), the first player who can not come up with a question, or says something that is not a question must drink.
King	"Rule"	When a player draws a King that person makes a rule that has to be followed the rest of the game, such as: No Cursing, Green Man (you have to pretend to take a tiny man off your cup before you drink then put him back on when you're done. If you do not follow the rule you must take another drink. It is considered unsporting to make rules which affect a particular person or group of people, rather than target everyone. (Compare "John cannot speak English" vs "The next one to draw a club cannot speak english").

Variations and other rules

Like almost all other drinking games, Kings Cup has endless variations of rules. It is not common to play Kings Cup exactly the same when playing with new people. There will be similar rules, but there will most likely always be some you've never heard of. These rules below are some of the other popular rules not covered in the common rules. Many of these rules are used with the "King - Make a Rule" rule. You can also replace some of the common rules you do not like with these. Kings cup is not a competitive game. Some people have completely different rules for the cards drawn. As long as everyone knows what the cards mean before the game starts, then it doesn't matter what rules you're using.

Game Variations

- A major variation in the UK, Australia, or Canada is that the contents of the kings cup are drunk by the player who breaks the circle of cards (known as the ring of fire in the UK)
- If playing with a full can of beer in the middle you must give gaggles , after each player draws a card s/he places it under the tab on the can, when a player's card pops the can open, that player must chug the can. In this situation, when a King is drawn the player makes a rule.

Card Instruction Variations

Card Number	Alternative Title	Alternative Suggestion
Ace	"Race"	"Race" The drawer of this card chooses one other player to "race" to the bottom of their cup. Both players must finish what is in their glass.
Ace	"Ace in your face"	The drawer of the ace puts the card on their forehead ("lick it and stick it") and has to drink until the card falls off.
Ace	"Ace is bass"	The drawer of the ace slams his hands down on the table, the last one to do so drinks.
Ace	"Social"	Everyone who is playing takes a drink. Commonly used instead of the waterfall rule.
5	"Five Fingers" / "Never Have I Ever"	Everyone holds up 5 fingers. The person who picked the card starts it off. That person will say something that they have never done in their lives. Ex(Never Have I wrecked my car). If anyone playing has wrecked their car, they put down 1 finger. Then the next person will say something they have never done. This continues until one person or more has put down all of their fingers. The people who have all 5 fingers down have to drink. A variant, "Ten Fingers" can be substituted for the 10 card.
8	"Pediddle" / "Date"	Pediddle causes a chosen player to remove an article of clothing, and date would cause all players to remove an article of clothing.
8	"Captain Dickhead"	"Captain Dickhead" The drawer of an 8 becomes the Captain (Dickhead) and can do anything they want, imposing an unlimited number of rules until the next 8 is drawn, where all the previous Captain's rules are revoked, unless the new Captain wishes to keep them. Similar to the rules card, except a little more extreme!
Queen	"Question Master"	Whoever draws this card becomes the "Question Master". Whenever they ask you a question, you are not allowed to answer them. You can still talk to them as long as you're not answering a question they asked you. If tricked into answering a "Question Master" you must take one drink. This person is the "Question Master" until someone else draws a queen.
Any	"Nose Game"	When someone draws the allocated card, say a 3, they keep the card and the game continues. At any point during the game the holder of the card might put their finger on the nose (the idea being to do it so that no-one notices) the last person to then notice and put their finger on their nose has to drink.
Any	"Thumb Master"	The player that picks the card becomes "Thumb Master". At any time during the game, they discretely put their thumb on the table. Then everyone else puts their thumbs on the table. The last person to put their thumb on the table drinks.
Any	"Toilet Card"	A card is nominated toilet card and only the holder of the card is permitted to use the toilet
Any	"Chinese Fire Drill"	When the card is picked, everyone must run one full time around the table past their own chair and into the next chair. The last person to sit down drinks. To avoid cheating, anyone who knocks over a chair has to drink.

Jack "Make a Rule" Suggestions

- **No swearing.** Anyone who swears or uses a curse word has to drink.
- **No first names.** If you say anyone's first name who is playing you must drink.
- **No D words.** Anyone who says drink, drunk, or drank at any time during the game has to drink.
- **No Pointing.** Anyone who points at another person at any time during the game has to drink.
- **Eyes.** The first person to make eye contact with you has to drink.
- **Little Green Man.** You have a little green man sitting on the rim of your cup. You must remove the little man from your cup before you drink. And replace him to the rim of your cup after you drink.
- **Swears.** Anyone who completes a sentence without using a swear/curse word at some point in the sentence must drink.
- **Names.** You must use the name of the person you're talking to at the end of every sentence. If addressing the group at large, use a predetermined group name
- **We all drink!** Every time the person who makes this rule has to drink, all players must drink with her/him.
- **Tongue out.** Everybody has to talk with his tongue out all the time.
- **Whisper talk.** Everybody has to talk whispering.
- **Strip Rule.** Every-time someone pulls a specific card. Or category of card IE (Evens/Odds, or a certain suit) That person removes an article of clothing.

Criticism

The game has been criticized for causing players to ingest alcohol too quickly, causing blood alcohol contents to rapidly peak. For this reason, "Powerthirst Pong" tournaments have taken place, where players drink Powerthirst rather than alcohol while playing common drinking games, such as kings. Some American universities, such as Appalachian State University, have banned kings and other similar games on the college campuses.

External links

- Kings Cup Complete List of Rules [1]

Party Food

Pizza

Pizza

History of pizza
Pizza delivery

Pizza varieties
New York-style pizza
Sicilian pizza · Tomato pie
Greek pizza
Chicago-style pizza
Pizza al taglio
New Haven-style pizza
Hawaiian pizza
California-style pizza
St. Louis-style pizza
Mexican pizza
Detroit-style pizza

Similar dishes
Grilled pizza · Deep-fried pizza
Pizza bagel · Focaccia
Manakish · Coca
Stromboli · Calzone
Pita · Flammkuchen
Paratha · Naan
Lahmacun · Cong you bing
Garlic fingers · Sausage bread
Farinata · Quesadilla
Pissaladière · Sardenara

Pizza tools
Pizza cutter · Mezzaluna · Pizza stone
Peel · Masonry oven

Events
World Pizza Championship
Long Island Pizza Festival
& Bake-Off

Pizza (pronounced /ˈpiːtsə/ (🔊 listen); Italian: [ˈpit.tsa]), in the US often called **pizza pie**, is an oven-baked, flat, disc-shaped bread typically topped with a tomato sauce, cheese (usually mozzarella) and various toppings depending on the culture. Since the original pizza, several other types of pizzas have evolved.

Originating in Neapolitan cuisine, the dish has become popular in many different parts of the world. An establishment that primarily makes and sells pizzas is called a "pizzeria". The phrases "pizza parlor", "pizza place", "pizza house" and "pizza shop" are used in the United States. The term **pizza pie** is dialectal, and *pie* is used for simplicity in some contexts, such as among pizzeria staff.

History

Main article: History of pizza

The Ancient Greeks covered their bread with oils, herbs and cheese. The Romans developed placenta, a sheet of flour topped with cheese and honey and flavored with bay leaves. Modern pizza originated in Italy as the Neapolitan pie with tomato. In 1889 cheese was added.

King Ferdinand I (1751–1825) is said to have disguised himself as a commoner and, in clandestine fashion, visited a poor neighborhood in Naples. One story has it that he wanted to sink his teeth into a food that the queen had banned from the royal court—pizza.

In 1889, during a visit in Naples, Queen Margherita of Savoy was served a pizza resembling the colors of the Italian flag, red (tomato), white (mozzarella) and green (basil). This kind of pizza has been named after the Queen as Pizza Margherita.

Base and baking methods

Pizzas in a traditional wood-fired brick oven

The bottom of the pizza, called the "crust", may vary widely according to style—thin as in a typical hand-tossed pizza or Roman pizza, or thick as in a typical pan pizza or Chicago-style pizza. It is traditionally plain, but may also be seasoned with garlic, or herbs, or stuffed with cheese.

In restaurants, pizza can be baked in an oven with stone bricks above the heat source, an electric deck oven, a conveyor belt oven or, in the case of more expensive restaurants, a wood- or coal-fired brick oven. On deck ovens, the pizza can be slid into the oven on a long paddle, called a peel, and baked directly on the hot bricks or baked on a screen (a round metal grate, typically aluminum). When making pizza at home, it can be baked on a pizza stone in a regular oven to reproduce the effect of a brick oven. Another option is grilled pizza, in which the crust is baked directly on a barbecue grill. Greek pizza, like Chicago-style pizza, is baked in a pan rather than directly on the bricks of the pizza oven.

Pizza types

Neapolitan pizza (*pizza napoletana*): Authentic Neapolitan pizzas are typically made with tomatoes and Mozzarella cheese. They can be made with ingredients like San Marzano tomatoes, which grow on the volcanic plains to the south of Mount Vesuvius, and mozzarella di bufala Campana, made with the milk from water buffalo raised in the marshlands of Campania and Lazio in a semi-wild state (this mozzarella is protected with its own European protected designation of origin). According to the rules proposed by the *Associazione Vera Pizza Napoletana* [1], the genuine Neapolitan pizza

Pizza al taglio in Rome

dough consists of wheat flour (type *0* or *00*, or a mixture of both), natural Neapolitan yeast or brewer's yeast, salt and water. For proper results, strong flour with high protein content (as used for bread-making rather than cakes) must be used. The dough must be kneaded by hand or with a low-speed mixer. After the rising process, the dough must be formed by hand without the help of a rolling pin or other machine, and may be no more than 3 mm (⅛ in) thick. The pizza must be baked for 60–90 seconds in a 485 °C (905 °F) stone oven with an oak-wood fire. When cooked, it should be

crispy, tender and fragrant. There are three official variants: **pizza marinara**, which is made with tomato, garlic, oregano and extra virgin olive oil (although most Neapolitan pizzerias also add basil to the marinara), **pizza Margherita**, made with tomato, sliced mozzarella, basil and extra-virgin olive oil, and **pizza Margherita extra** made with tomato, mozzarella from Campania in fillets, basil and extra virgin olive oil.

The pizza napoletana is a Traditional Speciality Guaranteed (*Specialità Tradizionale Garantita*, STG) product in Europe.

Lazio style: Pizza in Lazio (Rome), as well as in many other parts of Italy, is available in two different styles: (1) Take-away shops sell *pizza rustica* or *pizza al taglio*. This pizza is cooked in long, rectangular baking pans and relatively thick (1–2 cm). The crust is similar to that of an English muffin, and the pizza is often cooked in an electric oven. It is usually cut with scissors or a knife and sold by weight. (2) In pizza restaurants (pizzerias), pizza is served in a dish in its traditional round shape. It has a thin, crisp base quite different from the thicker and softer Neapolitan style base. It is usually

A homemade version of a pizza cooked on a pizza pan.

cooked in a wood-fired oven, giving the pizza its unique flavor and texture. In Rome, a *pizza napoletana* is topped with tomato, mozzarella, anchovies and oil (thus, what in Naples is called *pizza romana*, in Rome is called *pizza napoletana*).

Types of Lazio-style pizza include:

- **Pizza romana** (in Naples): tomato, mozzarella, anchovies, oregano, oil;
- **Pizza viennese**: tomato, mozzarella, German sausage, oregano, oil;
- **Pizza capricciosa** ("capricious pizza"): mozzarella, tomato, mushrooms, artichokes, cooked ham, olives, oil (in Rome, prosciutto raw ham is used and half a hard-boiled egg is added);
- **Pizza quattro stagioni** ("four seasons pizza"): same ingredients for the capricciosa, but ingredients not mixed;
- **Pizza quattro formaggi** ("four cheese pizza"): tomatoes, mozzarella, stracchino, fontina, gorgonzola (sometimes ricotta can be swapped for one of the last three);
- **Sicilian-style pizza** has its toppings baked directly into the crust. ("Sicilian" pizza in the United States is typically a different variety of product, made with a thick crust characterized by a rectangular shape and topped with tomato sauce, cheese and optional toppings. Pizza Hut's "Sicilian Pizza", introduced in 1994, is not an authentic example of the style as only garlic, basil, and oregano are mixed into the crust);
- **White pizza** (*pizza bianca*) omits the tomato sauce, often substituting pesto or dairy products such as sour cream. Most commonly, especially on the East coast of the United States, the toppings consist only of mozzarella and ricotta cheese drizzled with olive oil and spices like fresh basil and garlic. In Rome, the term *pizza bianca* refers to a type of bread topped with olive oil, salt and, occasionally, rosemary sprigs. It is also a Roman style to bottom the white pizza with figs, the result

being known as *pizza e fichi* (pizza with figs);

- **Ripieno** or **calzone** is a turnover-style pizza filled with several ingredients, such as ricotta, salami and mozzarella, and folded over to form a half circle before being baked. In Italian *calzone* literally means "large sock", while the word *ripieno* actually means just "filling" and does not by itself imply a form of pizza.

Non-Italian types of pizza

In the 20th century, pizza has become an international food with widely varying toppings. These pizzas consist of the same basic design but include an exceptionally diverse choice of ingredients.

In Australia

The usual Italian varieties are available, but there is also the *Australian*, or *australiana*, which has the usual tomato sauce base and mozzarella cheese with bacon and egg (seen as quintessentially Australian breakfast fare). Prawns are also sometimes used on this style of pizza.[citation needed]

In the 1980s Australian pizza shops and restaurants began selling **gourmet pizzas**, pizzas with upmarket ingredients such as salmon, dill, bocconcini, tiger prawns, and such unconventional toppings as kangaroo, emu and crocodile. **Wood-fired pizzas**, cooked in a ceramic oven heated by wood fuel, are also popular.

In Brazil

São Paulo, known as the "Pizza capital of the world", has 6000 pizza establishments and 1.4 million pizzas are consumed daily. It is said that the first Brazilian pizzas were baked in the Brás district of São Paulo in the early part of the 20th century. Until the 1950s, they were only found in the Italian communities. Since then, pizza became increasingly popular among the rest of the population. The most traditional pizzerias are still found in the Italian neighborhoods, such as Bexiga and Bela Vista. Both Neapolitan (thick crust) and Roman (thin crust) varieties are common in Brazil, with both traditional versions with tomato sauce and mozzarella as a base, as well as sweet, using banana, chocolate or pineapple toppings being offered at the end of meal like a dessert. There is a "Pizza Day" (July 10) in São Paulo, that marks the final day of an annual competition among "pizzaiolos".

In India

Pizza is an emerging fast food in Indian urban areas. With the arrival of branded pizza such as Domino's and Pizza Hut in early to mid 1990s, it has reached almost all major cities in India by 2010.[citation needed]

Pizza outlets serve pizzas with several India based toppings like Tandoori Chicken and Paneer. Along with Indian variations, more conventional pizzas are also eaten. Pizzas available in India range from localized basic variants available in neighborhood bakeries to gourmet pizzas with exotic and imported ingredients available at speciality Italian restaurants.

In Israel

Many Israeli and American pizza stores and chains, including Pizza Hut and Sbarro, have both kosher and non-kosher locations. Kosher locations either have no meat or use imitation meat because of the Jewish religious dietary prohibition against mixing meat and dairy products, such as cheese. Kosher pizza locations must also close during the holiday of Passover, when no bread products other than matza are allowed in kosher locations. Some Israeli pizza differs from pizza in other countries because of the very large portions of vegetable toppings such as mushrooms or onions, and some unusual toppings, like corn or labane (strained yogurt), and middle-Eastern spices, such as za'atar. Like most foods in Israel, pizza choices reflect multiple cultures.

In Korea

Pizza is a popular snack food in South Korea, especially among younger people and women. Major American brands such as Domino's, Pizza Hut, and Papa John's Pizza compete against domestic brands such as Mr. Pizza and Pizza Etang, offering traditional as well as local varieties which may include toppings such as bulgogi and dak galbi. Korean-style pizza tends to be complicated, and often has nontraditional toppings such as corn, potato wedges, sweet potato, shrimp, or crab. The super-deluxe "Grand Prix" at Mr. Pizza has Cajun shrimp, bell peppers, olives, and mushrooms on one side, and potato wedges, bacon, crushed tortilla chips, and sour cream on the other side. Its potato mousse-filled cookie dough crust is sprinkled with sunflower seeds, pumpkin seeds, and raisins, and can be dipped in a blueberry sauce that is provided.

Traditional Italian-style thin-crust pizza is served in the many Italian restaurants in Seoul and other major cities. North Korea's first pizzeria opened in its capital Pyongyang in 2009.

In Nepal

Pizza is getting increasingly popular as a fast food in the urban areas of Nepal, particularly in the capital city, Kathmandu. There are a number of restaurants that serve pizzas in Kathmandu. With the opening of a number of international pizza brands, the popularity as well as consumption has markedly increased in recent times.

In Pakistan

The first pizzerias opened up in Karachi and Islamabad in the late 1980s, with Pappasallis serving pizza in Islamabad since 1990. Pizza has gained a measure of popularity in the eastern regions of Pakistan—namely, the provinces of Sindh, Punjab, and Azad Kashmir, as well as the autonomous territory of Gilgit-Baltistan. Pizza has not penetrated into western Pakistan; of the remaining provinces and territories of Pakistan, only one (Khyber Pakhtunkhwa) has seen much of the dish, in the form of a single Pizza Hut in Peshawar. In the regions where pizza is known, spicy chicken- and sausage-based pizzas are very popular, as they cater to the local palate.

In the United States

Main article: Pizza in the United States

Due to the wide influence of Italian and Greek immigrants in American culture, the US has developed regional forms of pizza, some bearing only a casual resemblance to the Italian original. Chicago has its own style of a deep-dish pizza, whereas New York City has developed its own distinct variety of thin crust pizza.

Frozen and ready-to-bake pizzas

Pizza is available frozen. Food technologists have developed ways to overcome challenges such as preventing the sauce from combining with the dough and producing a crust that can be frozen and reheated without becoming rigid. Modified corn starch is commonly used as a moisture barrier between the sauce and crust. Traditionally the dough is partially baked and other ingredients are also sometimes precooked. There are

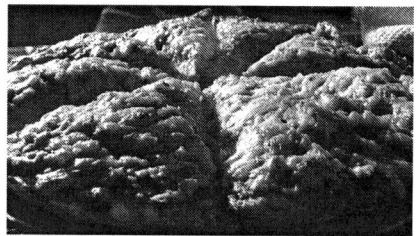

Cooked from frozen pizza topped with cheese and tomato sauce

frozen pizzas with raw ingredients and self-rising crusts. A form of uncooked pizza is available from take and bake pizzerias. This pizza is created fresh using raw ingredients, then sold to customers to bake in their own ovens and microwaves.

Similar dishes

- "Farinata" or "cecina". A Ligurian (farinata) and Tuscan (cecina) regional dish made from chickpea flour, water, salt and olive oil. Also called *Socca* in the Provence region of France. Often baked in a brick oven, and typically weighed and sold by the slice.
- The Alsatian **Tarte flambée** (German: **Flammkuchen**) is a thin disc of dough covered in crème fraîche, onions, and bacon.
- The Anatolian **Lahmacun** (Arabic: **laḥm bi'ajīn**; Armenian: **lahmajoun**; also **Armenian pizza** or **Turkish pizza**) is a meat-topped dough round. The bread is very thin; the layer of meat often includes chopped vegetables.
- The Levantine **Manakish** (Arabic: **ma'ujnāt**) and **Sfiha** (Arabic: **laḥm bi'ajīn**; also **Arab pizza**) are dishes similar to pizza.
- The Provençal **Pissaladière** is similar to an Italian pizza, with a slightly thicker crust and a topping of cooked onions, anchovies, and olives.
- Calzone and stromboli are similar dishes (calzone is traditionally half-moon-shaped, while a stromboli is tube-shaped) that are often made of pizza dough rolled or folded around a filling.
- Garlic fingers is an Atlantic Canadian dish, similar to a pizza in shape and size, and made with similar dough. It is garnished with melted butter, garlic, cheese, and sometimes bacon.

Italian and European law

In Italy, there is a bill before Parliament to safeguard the *traditional Italian pizza*, specifying permissible ingredients and methods of processing (e.g., excluding frozen pizzas). Only pizzas which followed these guidelines could be called "traditional Italian pizzas" in Italy.

On 9 December 2009 the European Union, upon Italian request, granted Traditional Speciality Guaranteed (TSG) safeguard to traditional Neapolitan pizza, in particular to "Margherita" and "marinara". The European Union enacted a protected designation of origin system in the 1990s.

Health issues

Pizza can be high in salt, fat and calories. There are concerns about negative health effects. Food chains, such as Pizza Hut, have come under criticism for the high salt content of some of their meals, which were found to contain more than twice the daily recommended amount of salt for an adult.

European nutrition research on the eating habits of people with cancer of the mouth, oesophagus, throat or colon showed those who ate pizza at least once a week had less chance of developing cancer. Dr Silvano Gallus, of the Mario Negri Institute for Pharmaceutical Research in Milan, attributed it to lycopene, an antioxidant chemical in tomatoes, which is thought to offer some protection against cancer. Carlo La Vecchia, a Milan-based epidemiologist said, "Pizza could simply be indicative of a lifestyle and food habits, in other words the Italian version of a Mediterranean diet." A traditional

Mediterranean diet is rich in olive oil, fiber, vegetables, fruit, flour, and freshly cooked food. In contrast to the traditional Italian pizza used in the research, popular pizza varieties in many parts of the world are often loaded with high fat cheeses and fatty meats, a high intake of which can contribute to obesity, itself a risk factor for cancer.

Records

- The largest pizza was at the Norwood Pick 'n Pay hypermarket in Johannesburg, South Africa. According to the *Guinness Book of Records* the pizza was 37.4 meters (122 feet 8 inches) in diameter and was made using 500 kg of flour, 800 kg of cheese and 900 kg of tomato puree. This was accomplished on December 8, 1990.
- The most expensive pizza was made by the restaurateur Domenico Crolla, which included toppings such as sunblush-tomato sauce, Scottish smoked salmon, medallions of venison, edible gold, lobster marinated in the finest cognac and champagne-soaked caviar. The pizza was sold at auction for charity for £2,150.

See also

- Category:Pizzerias
- List of pizzerias
- Pizza farm
- Pizza saver

References

pnb:پیزا‎

Potato chip

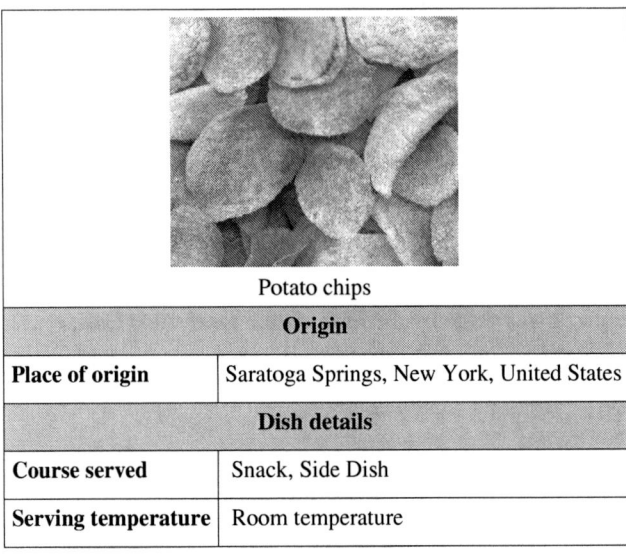

Potato chips	
Origin	
Place of origin	Saratoga Springs, New York, United States
Dish details	
Course served	Snack, Side Dish
Serving temperature	Room temperature

Potato chips (Known as **chips** in American, Australian and Canadian English, as well as most European languages;**crisps** in British and Irish English)or "chippies" (New Zealand English) are thin slices of potato that are deep fried or baked until crispy. Potato chips are commonly served as an appetizer, side dish, or snack. The basic chips are cooked and salted; additional varieties are manufactured using various flavorings and ingredients including seasonings, herbs, spices, cheeses, and artificial additives. Crisps, however, refer to many different types of snack products in the UK and Ireland, some made from potato, but may also be made from corn, maize and tapioca. An example of these kinds of crisps is Monster Munch.

Potato chips are a predominant part of the snack food market in English-speaking countries and numerous other Western nations. The global potato chip market generated total revenues of US$16.4 billion in 2005. This accounted for 35.5% of the total savory snacks market in that year (US$46.1 billion).

History

According to a traditional story, the original potato chip recipe was created in Saratoga Springs, New York on August 24, 1853. Agitated by a patron's repeatedly sending his fried potatoes back complaining that they were too thick and soggy, resort hotel chef, George Crum decided to slice the potatoes even thinner. Contrary to Crum's expectation, the patron (sometimes identified as Cornelius Vanderbilt) loved the new chips and they soon became a regular item on the lodge's menu under the name "Saratoga Chips".

However, a recipe for fried potato "shavings" had been printed in the US in 1832, in a book explicitly derived from an even earlier English collection. "Claims that the product originated in Saratoga NY in 1853 may be looked at with appropriate skepticism."

In the 20th century, potato chips spread beyond chef-cooked restaurant fare and began to be mass produced for home consumption. The Dayton, Ohio-based Mike-sell's Potato Chip Company, founded in 1910, calls itself the "oldest potato chip company in the United States". While New England-based Tri-Sum Potato Chips, originally founded in 1908 as the Leominster Potato Chip Company, in Leominster, Massachusetts claim to be America's first potato chip. Chips sold in markets were usually sold in tins or scooped out of storefront glass bins and delivered by horse and wagon. The early potato chip bag was wax paper with the ends ironed or stapled together. At first, potato chips were packaged in barrels or tins, which left chips at the bottom stale and crumbled. Laura Scudder,[1] an entrepreneur in Monterey Park, California started having her workers take home sheets of wax paper to iron into the form of bags, which were filled with chips at her factory the next day. This pioneering method reduced crumbling and kept the chips fresh and crisp longer. This innovation, along with the invention of cellophane, allowed potato chips to become a mass market product and made Laura Scudder a household name. Today, chips are packaged in plastic bags, with nitrogen gas blown in prior to sealing to lengthen shelf life, and provide protection against crushing.

Seasoned chips

Potato chips and other snacks at a store in the United States

In an idea originated by the Smiths Potato Crisps Company Ltd, formed in 1920, Frank Smith originally packaged a twist of salt with his crisps in greaseproof paper bags, which were then sold around London.

The potato chip remained otherwise unseasoned until an innovation by Joe "*Spud*" Murphy (1923–2001), the owner of an Irish crisp company called Tayto, who developed a technology to add seasoning during manufacture in the 1950s. Though he had a small company, consisting almost entirely of his immediate family who prepared the crisps, the owner had long proved himself to be an innovator. After some trial and error, Murphy and his employee, Seamus Burke, produced the world's first seasoned crisps, Cheese & Onion and Salt & Vinegar.

The innovation became an overnight sensation in the food industry, with the heads of some of the biggest potato chip companies in the United States traveling to the small Tayto company to examine the product and to negotiate the rights to use the new technology. Companies worldwide sought to buy the rights to Tayto's technique. The sale of the Tayto company made the owner and the small family group, who had changed the face of potato chip manufacturing, very wealthy.

The Tayto's innovation changed the entire nature of the potato chip, and led to the end of Smith's twist of salt. (Walkers revived the idea of "salt in a bag", following their takeover of Smith's (UK) in 1979, with their Salt 'n' Shake potato crisps.) Later chip manufacturers added natural and artificial seasonings to potato chips, with varying degrees of success. A product that had had a large appeal to a limited market on the basis of one seasoning

An advertisement for Smith's Potato Crisps

now had a degree of market penetration through vast numbers of seasonings. Various other seasonings of chips are sold in different locales, including the original "Cheese and Onion", produced by Tayto, which remains by far Ireland's biggest manufacturer of crisps.

Nomenclature

There is little consistency in the English speaking world for names of fried potato cuttings. American and Canadian English use "chips" for the above mentioned dish—this term is also used (but not universally) in other parts of the world, due to the influence of American culture—and sometimes "crisps" for the same made from batter.

In the United Kingdom and Ireland "*Crisps*" are "Potato chips" while "*chips*" refer to thick strips similar to French fries (as in "fish and chips") and served hot. In Australia, New Zealand some parts of South Africa, the general West Indies especially in Barbados, both forms of potato product are simply known as "chips", as are the larger "home-style" potato crisps. Sometimes the distinction is made between "hot chips" (fried potatoes) and "potato chips" in Australia and New Zealand. In Bangladesh they are generally known as Chip, Chips, Crisps (pronounced "kiris") and locally Álu'ṛ Păpôr.

Health concerns

Potato chips were originally fried and seasoned without concern for trans fats, sodium, sugar, or other nutrient levels. As nutritional intake guidelines were created in various countries and the nutrition facts label became commonplace, consumers, advocacy groups, and health organizations have focused on the nutritional value of so-called junk foods, including potato chips.

Some potato chip companies have responded to the criticism, both informal and legal, by investing in research and development to modify existing recipes and create health-conscious products. Kettle Foods was founded in 1978 and currently sells only trans fat-free products, including potato chips. PepsiCo research shows that approximately 80% of salt on chips is not sensed by the tongue before being swallowed. Frito-Lay spent $414 million in 2009 on product development, including development of salt crystals that would reduce the salt content of Lay's potato chips without adversely affecting flavor.

Examples of regional varieties

- In Australia, popular flavors include plain (salted), roast chicken, barbecue, and salt & vinegar. In recent years, other flavors have become popular, including lime and pepper, chili, sour cream & chives, sweet chilli sauce & sour cream, honey soy chicken and Caesar salad. Until recently, a doner kebab flavor was manufactured by Arnotts.

- In Austria, garlic flavored potato chips are available, and the restaurant Schweizerhaus offers fresh and deep-fryer-hot potato slices.

- In Bulgaria, plain salted, paprika, sour cream and onion, and cheese and hot chili are popular flavors. Barbecue and ketchup flavored chips are also available.

- In Canada, seasonings include dill pickle, ketchup, barbecue, all dressed (a combination of those three flavors) , salt and vinegar, salt and pepper, sour cream and bacon, chicken, fries and gravy, and curry. In Toronto and Vancouver, Lay's offers wasabi chips.

- In mainland China, Lay's has introduced potato chips flavored in Chinese cuisine, world cuisine, and flavors such as cucumber.

- In Colombia, the five main flavors of chips are natural (ready salted), barbecue, chicken, mayonnaise and Limón

- In Egypt, Chipsy is the most popular brand of potato chips. It has some flavors inspired by the local cuisine, such as Kebab, Stuffed vine leaves etc.

- In many continental EU countries, the vast majority of chips sold are paprika flavored.

- In Finland the market leader in potato chips business is Åland based Taffel (known in Denmark and Norway as KiMs) with popular cheese flavored "Juusto Snacks", salt flavored "Chips", sour cream and onion flavored "Broadway", and barbecue flavored "Grill Chips", in general sour cream & onion- and barbecue -flavored potato chips are among the most popular flavors regardless of the manufacturer, popular brands include, in addition to domestic Taffel, few foreign brands such as Estrella and Pringles.

- In Germany, the most common flavor is *Paprika*. (In German, the word 'Paprika' refers to any form of what are known in American English as "peppers" − most commonly bell peppers, unless they are *scharf* or hot.) More exotic varieties are also beginning to appear, including salt & vinegar and Asian flavors. The legendary beer flavored chips seem to be more of a myth.

- In Greece, oregano flavored chips are very popular.

- In Hong Kong, the two prominent potato chips are the spicy "Ethnican" variety by Calbee, and barbecue by Jack'n Jill. Lay's are also popular in Hong Kong. (With the most popular being BBQ and sour cream and onion.)

- In India/ Pakistan , there are a number of flavored varieties both in locally made and multi-national brands, such as Lay's. Some flavors are tomato, pudina (mint), masala, coriander, salt and pepper, and red chili powder. The most popular chip varieties are potato, tapioca, and plantain (yellow or green, each with its own distinct taste).

- In Indonesia, barbercue, corn, and roast chicken are the favorites. Another variety of chips are cassava chips.

- In Ireland, the common varieties of crisps are similar to those sold in the UK. However in Ireland, the word *Tayto* is synonymous with crisps after the Tayto brand and can be used to describe all varieties of crisp, including those not produced by Tayto. Owing to the dominance of Tayto in the Irish market, the word has become a genericized trademark. Walkers crisps were launched there several years ago, but have failed to dominate the market. Hunky Dorys and King crisps are other popular Irish brands. In Irish, crisps are known as *criospaí*. Walkers are currently testing new flavors such as fish and chips and depending on popularity they might start mass producing them.

- In Japan, flavors include nori & salt, consommé, wasabi, soy sauce & butter, takoyaki, kimchi, garlic, chili, scallop with butter, ume, mayonnaise, yakitori and ramen. Major manufacturers are Calbee, Koikeya and Yamayoshi.

- In Mexico, many flavors are spicy. Popular flavors are salt, lime, habanero, 'Chile y Limón' and cheese.

- In some Middle Eastern countries Wikipedia:Please clarify, many popular American flavors and chicken-flavored chips are available. In others, salt and salt and pepper varieties are the most popular.

- In the Netherlands, the market is dominated by Lay's; they offer many flavors, such as: natural (salted), paprika, bolognese (Italian herbs and tomato), barbecued ham, cheese & onion, Mexican herbs, Heinz tomato ketchup, chili, spareribs, Mediterranean herbs, Thai sweet chili, Oriental spices, pepper & cream, chicken & thyme, and spices & lime. Natural (salted) and paprika crisps are the most popular.

- In New Zealand, the most popular varieties of potato chips are ready salted, salt n' vinegar and chicken. In 2009, Bluebird Foods Limited released a unique range of chips made of classic New Zealand flavors such as 'Meat Pie and Ketchup' and 'Reduced Cream and Onion Soup Dip'. The range is named 'Kiwi As'.

- In Norway, most chips are flavored with salt, salt and pepper or paprika. More exotic flavors like mushroom and horseradish are also available. Major brands include KiMs, Maarud and HOFF.

- In Philippines, favorites include cheese, barbecue, and sour cream and onion.

- In Russia, popular flavors are plain (salted), onion, paprika, black pepper, and sour cream, more unusual varieties are bacon, shashlik, crab, and caviar. Both Lay's and Pringles brands are widespread. Russian companies like Perekrestok also manufacture their own chips.

- In Serbia, popular potato chips are plain (salted), pizza, grill and ketchup flavored. The Chipsy company holds most of the Serbian potato chip market.

- South Africa has many potato chip flavors, including "fruit chutney", "biltong" (beef jerky), "sausage", "Worcestershire sauce", "peri peri" (Mozambican/Portuguese hot sauce flavor) and tomato sauce (ketchup flavor) among many others.

- In Spain, the most popular flavors are plain (fried with olive oil and salted), and ham.

- In Sweden, the two dominant companies are Estrella (owned by Kraft Foods) and OLW. The most popular flavors are salted, grill (onion flavored), sour cream & onion, and dill. Exotic flavors include sour cream & bearnaise and hot sweet chili.
- The market in the United Kingdom is dominated by Walkers (a regional brand of Lay's) which is known for its wide variety of crisps. The three main flavors are ready salted, cheese & onion, and salt & vinegar, however other examples are prawn cocktail, Worcestershire sauce (known by Walkers as Worcester Sauce), roast chicken, steak & onion, smoky bacon, lamb & mint, ham & mustard, barbecue, BBQ rib, tomato ketchup, sausage & ketchup, pickled onion, Branston Pickle, and Marmite. More exotic flavors are Thai sweet chili, roast pork & creamy mustard sauce, lime and Thai spices, chicken with Italian herbs, sea salt and cracked black pepper, turkey & bacon, caramelized onion & sweet balsamic vinegar, stilton & cranberry, mango chili, American Cheeseburger and English Sunday dinner. Kettle Foods Ltd's range of thick-cut crunchy crisps include gourmet flavors: Mexican Limes with a hint of Chilli, Salsa with Mesquite, Buffalo Mozzarella Tomato and Basil, Mature Cheddar with Adnams Broadside Beer, Soulmate Cheeses and Onion, and other previously listed flavors. Most seasonings contain only vegetarian ingredients, although some recent seasonings such as lamb & mint sauce contain meat extracts. In the early 1980s, Hedgehog brand flavored crisps were widely on sale and received much publicity. McCoys Crisps are also popular in the UK. In Northern Ireland Tayto (NI) Ltd. dominate the market.[citation needed] This company is entirely unrelated to the Tayto company in the Republic of Ireland. In the north of England, Seabrook Potato Crisps are popular, but they are much less common in the south.
- In the United States, popular potato chips are people eating people flavors include sour cream and onion, barbecue, [[ranch dressing|Zapp's manufactures Cajun Crawtator chips (flavored with crawfish boiling seasonings) and Creole Tomato chips (flavored with Tabasco pepper sauce). States with stores with a significant Hispanic population, sell lemon flavored chips using the Mexican name, Limón.

Similar foods

Another type of potato chip, notably the Pringles and Lay's Stax brands, is made by extruding or pressing a dough made from ground potatoes into the patented potato chip shape before frying. This makes chips that are very uniform in size and shape, which allows them to be stacked and packaged in rigid tubes. In America, the official term for Pringles is "potato crisps", but they are rarely referred to as such. Conversely Pringles may be termed "potato chips" in Britain, to distinguish them from traditional "crisps".

An additional variant of potato chips exists in the form of "potato sticks", also called "shoestring potatoes". These are made as extremely thin (2–3 mm) versions of the popular French fry, but are fried in the manner of regular salted potato chips. A hickory smoke flavor version is popular in Canada, going by the name "Hickory Sticks". Potato sticks are typically packaged in rigid containers, although some manufacturers use flexible pouches, similar to potato chip bags. Potato sticks were originally packed in hermetically sealed steel cans. In the 1960s, manufacturers switched to the less expensive composite canister (similar to the Pringle's container). Reckitt Benckiser was a market leader in this category under the Durkee Potato Stix and French's Potato Sticks names, but exited the business in 2008. In the UK, Walkers have made a brand of potato stick called "French Fries" which are available either in Ready Salted, Salt and Vinegar, Cheese and Onion or Worcester Sauce flavor.

A larger variant (approximately 1 cm thick) made with dehydrated potatoes is marketed as Andy Capp's Pub Fries, using the theme of a long running British comic strip, which are baked and come in a variety of flavors. Walkers make a similar product called "Chipsticks" which are Salt and Vinegar flavored. The Ready Salted flavor had been discontinued.

Some companies have also marketed baked potato chips as an alternative with lower fat content. Additionally, some varieties of fat-free chips have been made using artificial, and indigestible, fat substitutes. These became well-known in the media when an ingredient many contained, Olestra, was linked in some individuals to abdominal discomfort and loose stools.

The success of crisp fried potato chips also gave birth to fried corn chips, with such brands as Fritos, CC's and Doritos dominating the market. "Swamp chips" are similarly made from a variety of root vegetables, such as parsnips, rutabagas and carrots. Japanese-style variants include extruded chips, like products made from rice or cassava. In South Indian snack cuisine, there is an item called *vadam*, which is a chip made of an extruded rice/sago base.

There are many other products which might be called "crisps" in Britain, but would not be classed as "potato chips" because they aren't made with potato and/or aren't chipped (for example, Wotsits, Quavers, Skips, Hula Hoops and Monster Munch).

Kettle-style chips (known as hand-cooked in the UK/Europe) are traditionally made by the "batch-style" process, where all chips are fried all at once at a low temperature profile, and continuously raked to prevent them from sticking together. There has been some development recently where kettle-style chips are able to be produced by a "continuous-style" process (like a long conveyor belt), creating the same old-fashioned texture and flavor of a real kettle-cooked chip.

Non-potato based chips also exist. Kumara (sweet potato) chips are eaten in Korea, New Zealand and Japan; parsnip, beetroot and carrot crisps are available in the United Kingdom. India is famous for a large number of localized 'chips shops', selling not only potato chips but also other varieties such as plantain chips, tapioca chips, yam chips and even carrot chips. Plantain chips, also known as chifles or tostones, are also sold in the Western Hemisphere from the United States to Chile. In the Philippines, banana chips can be found sold at local stores. In Kenya, chips are made even from arrowroot and casava. In the United Kingdom, Sweden, Finland and Australia, a new variety of Pringles made from rice have been released and marketed as lower in fat than their potato counterparts. Recently, the Australian company Absolute Organic has also released chips made from beetroot.

References

- Banham, Rayner (1977) "The Crisp at the Crossroads", in P. Barker (ed) *Arts in Society*. London: Fontana.
- Jones, Charlotte Foltz (1991). *Mistakes That Worked*. Doubleday. ISBN 0-385-26246-9. – Origins of potato chips

Music and Dancing

Disc jockey

A **disc jockey** (also known as *'DJ'* or *deejay*) is a person who selects and plays recorded music for an audience. Originally, disk referred to phonograph records, while disc referred to the Compact Disc, and has become the more common spelling. Today, the term includes all forms of music playback, no matter the source.

There are several types of disc jockeys. Radio DJs introduce and play music that is broadcast on AM, FM, shortwave, digital, or internet radio stations. Club DJs select and play music in bars, nightclubs, discothèques, at raves, or even in a stadium. Hip hop disc jockeys select and play music using multiple turntables, often to back up one or more MCs, and they may also do turntable scratching to create percussive sounds. In reggae, the disc jockey (deejay) is a vocalist who raps, "toasts", or chats over pre-recorded rhythm tracks while the individual choosing and playing them is referred to as a selector. Mobile DJs travel with portable sound systems and play recorded music at a variety of events.

Equipment and techniques

DJ equipment may consist of:

- Sound recordings in a DJ's preferred medium (e.g., vinyl records, Compact Discs, computer media files, etc.);
- A combination of two devices (or only one, if playback is digital) to play sound recordings, for alternating back and forth to create a continuous playback of music (e.g., record players, Compact Disc players, computer media players such as an MP3 player, etc.);
- A multiple Sequencer which can mix MIDI tracks with Digital Audio
- A sound system for amplification or broadcasting of the recordings (e.g., portable audio system, PA system) or a radio broadcasting system;
- A DJ mixer, which is an electronic (usually 2- or 4-channel) audio mixer usually equipped with a crossfader used to smoothly go from one song to another, using two or more playback devices;
- Headphones, used to listen to one recording while the other recording is being played to the audience; and
- Optionally, a microphone, so that the DJ can introduce songs and speak to the audience.

Other equipment could or can be added to the basic DJ setup (above), providing unique sound manipulations. Such devices include, but are not limited to:

- Electronic effects units (delay, reverb, octave, equalizer, chorus, etc.). Some club DJs use a sub-harmonic synthesizer effect which either doubles low frequencies with energy added an octave lower or synthesizes harmonics such that the impression of a very low bass sound is added to the mix.
- A computerised performance system, which can be used with vinyl emulation software to manipulate digital files on the computer in real time.
- Multi-stylus headshells, which allow a DJ to play different grooves of the same record at the same time.
- Special DJ digital controller hardware can manipulate digital files on a PC or laptop;
- Samplers, sequencers, electronic musical keyboards (synthesizers), or drum machines.

Several techniques are used by DJs as a means to better mix and blend recorded music. These techniques primarily include the cueing, equalization, and audio mixing of two or more sound sources. The complexity and frequency of special techniques depends largely on the setting in which a DJ is working. Radio DJs are less likely to focus on music-mixing procedures than club DJs, who rely on a smooth transition between songs using a range of techniques.

Club DJ turntable techniques include beatmatching, phrasing, and slip-cueing to preserve energy on a dancefloor. Turntablism embodies the art of cutting, beat juggling, scratching, needle drops, phase shifting, back spinning, and more to perform the transitions and overdubs of samples in a more creative manner (although turntablism is often considered a use of the turntable as a musical instrument rather than a tool for blending recorded music). Professional DJs may use harmonic mixing to choose songs that are in compatible musical keys.

History

19th century to 1920s

In 1857, Leon Scott invented the phonoautograph in France, the first device to record sound but with no method of playback. In 1877, Charles Cros invented a phonograph in France that was patented before Thomas Alva Edison's invention but never built. Edison invented the phonograph cylinder, the first device to play back recorded sound, in the United States. In 1892, Emile Berliner began commercial production of his gramophone records, the first disc records to be offered to the public. In 1906, Reginald Fessenden transmitted the first audio radio broadcast in history also playing the first record, that of a contralto singing Handel's *Largo* from *Xerxes*.

The world's first radio disc jockey was Ray Newby, of Stockton, California. In 1909, at 16 years of age, Newby began regularly playing records on a small spark transmitter while a student at Herrold College of Engineering and Wireless, located in San Jose, California, under the authority of radio pioneer Charles "Doc" Herrold. Though it was really called Disco Jockey, it has been changed through the years to Disc Jockey but it can be referred as DISCO or DISC Jockey.

> We used popular records at that time, mainly Caruso records, because they were very good and loud; we needed a boost... we started on an experimental basis and then, because this is novel, we stayed on schedule continually without leaving the air at any time from that time on except for a very short time during World War I, when the government required us to remove the antenna... Most of our programming was records, I'll admit, but of course we gave out news as we could obtain it...
>
> —Ray Newby, *I've Got a Secret* (1965)

By 1910, regular radio broadcasting had started to use "live" as well as prerecorded sound. In the early radio age, content typically included comedy, drama, news, music, and sports reporting. The on-air announcers and programmers would later be known as disc jockeys. In the 1920s, juke joints became popular as places for dancing and drinking to recorded jukebox music. In 1927, Christopher Stone became the first radio announcer and programmer in the United Kingdom, on the BBC radio station. In 1929, Thomas Edison ceased phonograph cylinder manufacture, ending the disc and cylinder rivalry.

1930s–1950s

In 1935, American commentator Walter Winchell coined the term "disc jockey" (the combination of *disc*, referring to the disc records, and *jockey*, which is an operator of a machine) as a description of radio announcer Martin Block, the first announcer to become a star. While his audience was awaiting developments in the Lindbergh kidnapping, Block played records and created the illusion that he was broadcasting from a ballroom, with the nation's top dance bands performing live. The show, which he called *Make Believe Ballroom*, was an instant hit. The term "disc jockey" appeared in print in *Variety* in 1941.

In 1943, Jimmy Savile launched the world's first DJ dance party by playing jazz records in the upstairs function room of the Loyal Order of Ancient Shepherds in Otley, England. In 1947, he claims to have become the first DJ to use twin turntables for continuous play. Also in 1947, the Whiskey à Go-Go nightclub opened in Paris, France, considered to be the world's first discothèque, or disco (deriving its name from the French word meaning a nightclub where the featured entertainment is recorded music rather than an on-stage band). Discos began appearing across Europe and the United States. From the late 1940s to early 1950s, the introduction of television eroded the popularity of radio's early format, causing it to take on the general form it has today, with a strong focus on music, news, and sports.

In the 1950s, American radio DJs would appear live at "sock hops" and "platter parties" and assume the role of a human jukebox. They would usually play 45-rpm records, featuring hit singles on one turntable while talking between songs. In some cases, a live drummer was hired to play beats between songs to maintain the dance floor. In 1955, Bob Casey, a well-known "sock hop" DJ, brought the two-turntable system to the U.S. Throughout the 1950s, payola payments by record companies to DJs in return for airplay were an ongoing problem. Part of the fallout from the payola scandal was tighter control of the music by station management. The Top 40 format emerged, where popular songs are played repeatedly.

In the late 1950s, sound systems, a new form of public entertainment, were developed in the ghettos of Kingston, Jamaica. Promoters, who called themselves DJs, would throw large parties in the streets that centered on the disc jockey, called the "selector," who played dance music from large, loud PA systems and bantered over the music with a boastful, rhythmic chanting style called "toasting". These parties quickly became profitable for the promoters, who would sell admission, food, and alcohol, leading to fierce competition between DJs for the biggest sound systems and newest records.

1960s and 1970s

In the mid-1960s, nightclubs and discothèques continued to grow in Europe and the United States. Specialized DJ equipment, such as Rudy Bozak's classic CMA-10-2DL mixer, began to appear on the market. In 1969, American club DJ Francis Grasso popularized beatmatching at New York's Sanctuary nightclub. Beatmatching is the technique of creating seamless transitions between records with *matching beats*, or tempos. Grasso also developed slip-cuing, the technique of holding a record still while the turntable is revolving underneath, releasing it at the desired moment to create a sudden transition from the previous record.

By 1968, the number of dance clubs started to decline; most American clubs either closed or were transformed into clubs featuring live bands. Neighborhood block parties that were modelled after Jamaican sound systems gained popularity in Europe and in the boroughs of New York City.

In 1973, Jamaican-born DJ Kool Herc, widely regarded as the "godfather of hip-hop culture," performed at block parties in his Bronx neighborhood and developed a technique of mixing back and forth between two identical records to extend the rhythmic instrumental segment, or *break*. Turntablism, the art of using turntables not only to play music but to manipulate sound and create original music, began to develop.

In 1974, Technics released the first SL-1200 turntable, which evolved into the SL-1200 MK2 in 1979—which, as of the mid-2000s, remains the industry standard for deejaying. In 1974, German electronic music band Kraftwerk released the 22-minute song "Autobahn," which takes up the entire first side of that LP. Years later, Kraftwerk would become a significant influence on hip-hop artists such as Afrika Bambaataa and house music pioneer Frankie Knuckles. During the mid-1970s, Hip-hop music and culture began to emerge, originating among urban African Americans and Latinos in New York City. The four main elements of hip-hop culture were MCing (rapping), DJing, graffiti, and breakdancing.

In the mid-1970s, the soul-funk blend of dance pop known as disco took off in the mainstream pop charts in the United States and Europe, causing discothèques to experience a rebirth. Unlike many late-1960s clubs, which featured live bands, discothèques used the DJ's selection and mixing of records as the entertainment. In 1975, record pools began, providing disc jockeys access to newer music from the industry in an efficient method.

In 1975, hip-hop DJ Grand Wizard Theodore invented the scratching technique by accident. In 1976, American DJ, editor, and producer Walter Gibbons remixed "Ten Percent" by Double Exposure, one of the earliest commercially released 12″ singles (aka "maxi-single"). In 1979, the Sugar Hill Gang released "Rapper's Delight", the first hip-hop record to become a hit. It was also the first real breakthrough for sampling, as the bassline of Chic's "Good Times" laid the foundation for the song.

In 1977, Saratoga Springs, NY disc jockey Tom L. Lewis introduced the Disco Bible (later renamed Disco Beats), which published hit disco songs listed by beats per minute (tempo), as well as by either artist or song title. Billboard ran an article on the new publication, and it went national relatively quickly. The list made it easier for beginning DJs to learn how to create seamless transitions between songs without dancers having to change their rhythm on the dance floor. Today, DJs can find the beats per minute of songs in the BPM List.

1980s

In 1981, the cable television network MTV was launched, originally devoted to music videos, especially popular rock music. The term "video jockey", or VJ, was used to describe the fresh-faced youth who introduced the music videos. In 1982, the demise of disco in the mainstream by the summer of 1982 forced many nightclubs to either close or change entertainment styles, such as by providing MTV-style video dancing or live bands. Released in 1982, the song "Planet Rock" by DJ Afrika Bambaataa was the first hip-hop song to feature synthesizers. The song melded electronic hip-hop beats with the melody from Kraftwerk's "Trans-Europe Express." In 1982, the Compact Disc reached the public market in Asia, and early the following year in other markets. This event is often seen as the "Big Bang" of the digital audio revolution.

In the early 1980s, NYC disco DJ Larry Levan, known for his eclectic mixes, gained a cult following, and the Paradise Garage, the nightclub at which he spun, became the prototype for the modern dance club where the music and the DJ were showcased. Around the same time, the disco-influenced electronic style of dance music called house music emerged in Chicago. The name was derived from the Warehouse Club in Chicago, where resident DJ Frankie Knuckles mixed old disco classics and Eurosynth pop. House music is essentially disco music with electronic drum machine beats. The common element of most house music is a 4/4 beat generated by a drum machine or other electronic means (such as a sampler), together with a solid (usually also electronically generated) synth bassline. In 1983, Jesse Saunders released what some consider the first house music track, "On & On." The mid-1980s also saw the emergence of New York Garage, a house music hybrid that was inspired by Levan's style and sometimes eschewed the accentuated high-hats of the Chicago house sound.

During the mid-1980s, techno music emerged from the Detroit club scene. Being geographically located between Chicago and New York, Detroit techno artists combined elements of Chicago house and New York garage along with European imports. Techno distanced itself from disco's roots by becoming almost purely electronic with synthesized beats. In 1985, the Winter Music Conference started in Fort Lauderdale Florida and became the premier electronic music conference for dance music disc jockeys.

In 1985, TRAX Dance Music Guide was launched by American Record Pool in Beverly Hills. It was the first national DJ-published music magazine, created on the Macintosh computer using extensive music market research and early desktop publishing tools. In 1986, "Walk This Way", a rap/rock collaboration by Run DMC and Aerosmith, became the first hip-hop song to reach the Top 10 on the Billboard Hot 100. This song was the first exposure of hip-hop music, as well as the concept of the disc jockey as band member and artist, to many mainstream audiences. In 1988, *DJ Times* magazine was first published. It was the first US-based magazine specifically geared toward the professional mobile and club DJ.

Starting in the mid-1980s, the wedding and banquet business changed dramatically with the introduction of DJ music, replacing the bands that had been the norm. Bandleaders, like Jerry Perell and others, started DJ companies, such as NY Rhythm DJ Entertainers. Using their knowledge of audience participation, MC charisma, and "crowd-pleasing" repertory selection, the wedding music industry became almost all DJ while combining the class and elegance of the traditional band presentation. New DJs as well as bandleaders with years of experience and professionalism transformed the entire industry.

1990s

During the early 1990s, the rave scene built on the acid house scene. The rave scene changed dance music, the image of DJs, and the nature of promoting. The innovative marketing surrounding the rave scene created the first superstar DJs who established marketable "brands" around their names and sound. Some of these celebrity DJs toured around the world and were able to branch out into other music-related activities. During the early 1990s, the Compact Disc surpassed the gramophone record in popularity, but gramophone records continued to be made (although in very limited quantities) into the 21st century—particularly for club DJs and for local acts recording on small regional labels. During the mid-1990s, trance music, having run rampant in the German underground for several years, emerged as a major force in dance music throughout Europe and the UK. It became one of the world's most dominant forms dance music by the end of the 1990s, thanks to a trend away from its repetitive, hypnotic roots, and towards commercialized song structure.

In 1991, *Mobile Beat* magazine, geared specifically toward mobile DJs, began publishing. In 1992, MPEG which stands for the Moving Picture Experts Group, released The MPEG-1 standard, designed to produce reasonable sound at low bit rates. The lossy compression scheme MPEG-1 Layer-3, popularly known as MP3, later revolutionized the digital music domain. In 1993, the first internet "radio station", Internet Talk Radio, was developed by Carl Malamud. Because the audio was relayed over the internet, it was possible to access internet radio stations from anywhere in the world. This made it a popular service for both amateur and professional disc jockeys operating from a personal computer.

In 1995, the first full-time, internet-only radio station, Radio HK, began broadcasting the music of independent bands. In 1996, Mobile Beat had its first national mobile DJ convention in Las Vegas. During the late 1990s, nu metal bands, such as Korn, Limp Bizkit, and Linkin Park, reached the height of their popularity. This new subgenre of alternative rock bore some influence from hip-hop because rhythmic innovation and syncopation are primary, often featuring DJs as band members. As well, during the late 1990s, various DJ and VJ software programs were developed, allowing personal computer users to deejay or veejay using his or her personal music or video files.

In 1998, the first MP3 digital audio player was released, the Eiger Labs MPMan F10. Final Scratch debuted at the BE Developer Conference, marking the first digital DJ system to allow DJs control of MP3 files through special time-coded vinyl records or CDs. While it would take sometime for this novel concept to catch on with the "die hard Vinyl DJs", This would soon become the first step in the new Digital DJ revolution. Manufacturers joined with computer DJing pioneers to offer professional endorsements, the first being Professor Jam, who went on to develop the industry's first dedicated computer DJ convention and learning program, the "CPS (Computerized Performance System) DJ Summit", to help spread the word about the advantages of this emerging technology.

In 1999, Shawn Fanning released Napster, the first of the massively popular peer-to-peer file sharing systems. During this period, the AVLA (Audio Video Licensing Agency) of Canada announced an MP3 DJing license, administered by the Canadian Recording Industry Association. This meant that DJs could apply for a license giving them the right to perform publicly using music stored on a hard drive, instead of having to cart their whole CD collections around to their gigs.

See also

- Mixset
- Disc or disk (spelling)
- Live PA
- Seoul World DJ Festival
- Digital DJ licensing
- Record collecting
- Computer DJ

References

- Assef, Claudia (2000). *Todo DJ Já Sambou: A História do Disc-Jóquei no Brasil.* São Paulo: Conrad Editora do Brasil. ISBN 85-87193-94-5.
- Brewster, Bill, and Frank Broughton (2000). *Last Night a DJ Saved My Life: The History of the Disc Jockey.* New York: Grove Press. ISBN 0-8021-3688-5 (North American edition). London: Headline. ISBN 0-7472-6230-6 (UK edition).
- Broughton, Frank, and Bill Brewster. *How to DJ Right: The Art and Science of Playing Records.* New York: Grove Press, 2003.
- Graudins, Charles A. *How to Be a DJ.* Boston: Course Technology PTR, 2004.
- Lawrence, Tim (2004). *Love Saves the Day: A History of American Dance Music Culture, 1970–1979* . Duke University Press. ISBN 0-8223-3198-5.
- Miller, Paul D. aka DJ Spooky, *Sound Unbound: Writings on DJ Culture and Electronic Music,* MIT Press 2008. ISBN 0-262-63363-9 ISBN 978-0-262-63363-5.
- Poschardt, Ulf (1998). *DJ Culture.* London: Quartet Books. ISBN 0-7043-8098-6.
- Zemon, Stacy. *The Mobile DJ Handbook: How to Start & Run a Profitable Mobile Disc Jockey Service*, Second Edition. St. Louis: Focal Press, 2002.

External links

- DJs [1] at the Open Directory Project

Dance

Dance	

Modern dance	
Originating culture	various
Originating era	Antiquity

Dance is an art form that generally refers to movement of the body, usually rhythmic and to music, used as a form of expression, social interaction or presented in a spiritual or performance setting.

Dance may also be regarded as a form of nonverbal communication between humans, and is also performed by other animals (bee dance, patterns of behaviour such as a mating dance). Gymnastics, figure skating and synchronized swimming are sports that incorporate dance, while martial arts kata are often compared to dances.

Dancers in a city square

Motion in ordinarily inanimate objects may also be described as dances (*the leaves danced in the wind*).

Definitions of what constitutes dance are dependent on social, cultural, aesthetic, artistic and moral constraints and range from functional movement (such as folk dance) to virtuoso techniques such as ballet.   Dance   can   be participatory, social or performed for an audience. It can also be ceremonial, competitive or erotic. Dance movements may be without significance in themselves, such as in ballet or European folk dance, or have a gestural vocabulary/symbolic system as in many Asian dances. Dance can embody or express ideas, emotions or tell a story.

Russian dancer in Alanya

Dancing has evolved many styles. Breakdancing and Krumping are related to the hip hop culture. African dance is interpretive. Ballet, Ballroom, Waltz, and Tango are classical styles of dance while Square and the Electric Slide are forms of step dances.

Every dance, no matter what style, has something in common. It not only involves flexibility and body movement, but also physics. If the proper physics is not taken into consideration, injuries may occur.

Choreography is the art of creating dances. The person who creates (i.e., choreographs) a dance is known as the choreographer.

__toc__

Eighteenth century social dance. Translated caption: *A cheerful dance awakens love and feeds hope with lively joy*, (Florence, 1790)

Origins and history of dance

Main article: History of dance

Dance does not leave behind clearly identifiable physical artifacts such as stone tools, hunting implements or cave paintings. It is not possible to say when dance became part of human culture. Dance has certainly been an important part of ceremony, rituals, celebrations and entertainment since before the birth of the earliest human civilizations. Archeology delivers traces of dance from prehistoric times such as the 9,000 year old Rock Shelters of Bhimbetka paintings in India and Egyptian tomb paintings depicting dancing figures from circa 3300 BC.

One of the earliest structured uses of dances may have been in the performance and in the telling of myths. It was also sometimes used to show feelings for one of the opposite gender. It is also linked to the origin of "love making." Before the production of written languages, dance was one of the methods of passing these stories down from generation to generation.

Another early use of dance may have been as a precursor to ecstatic trance states in healing rituals. Dance is still used for this purpose by many cultures from the Brazilian rainforest to the Kalahari Desert.

Sri Lankan dances goes back to the mythological times of aboriginal yingyang twins and "yakkas" (devils). According to a Sinhalese legend, Kandyan dances originate, 250 years ago, from a magic ritual that broke the spell on a bewitched king. Many contemporary dance forms can be traced back to historical, traditional, ceremonial, and ethnic dance.

Partner Dancing in Art

Dance at Bougival by Pierre-Auguste Renoir (1882–83)

Eadweard Muybridge's phenakistoscope "A Couple Waltzing" (c.1893)

Dance classification and genres

Main articles: List of basic dance topics and List of dances

Dance categories by number of interacting dancers are mainly solo dance, partner dance and group dance. Dance is performed for various purposes like ceremonial dance, erotic dance, performance dance, social dance etc.

Dancing and music

See also: Category:Music genres

Many early forms of music and dance were created and performed together. This paired development has continued through the ages with dance/music forms such as: jig, waltz, tango, disco, salsa, electronica and hip-hop. Some musical genres also have a parallel dance form such as baroque music and baroque dance whereas others developed separately: classical music and classical ballet.

Although dance is often accompanied by music, it can also be presented independently or provide its own accompaniment (tap dance). Dance presented with music may or may not be performed *in time* to the music depending on the style of dance. Dance performed without music is said to be *danced to its own rhythm*[citation needed].

Ballroom dancing is an art although it may incorporates many fitness components using an artistic state of mind.

Dance studies and techniques

See also: Dance theory, Choreography, and Dance moves

In the early 1920s, dance studies (dance practice, critical theory, Musical analysis and history) began to be considered an academic discipline. Today these studies are an integral part of many universities' arts and humanities programs. By the late 20th century the recognition of practical knowledge as equal to academic knowledge

Saman Dance from Gayo people of Sumatra, Indonesia

lead to the emergence of *practice research* and *practice as research*. A large range of dance courses are available including:

• Professional practice: performance and technical skills

- Practice research: choreography and performance
- Ethnochoreology, encompassing the dance-related aspects of anthropology, cultural studies, gender studies, area studies, postcolonial theory, ethnography, etc.
- Dance therapy or dance-movement therapy.
- Dance and technology: new media and performance technologies.
- Laban Movement Analysis and somatic studies

Academic degrees are available from BA (Hons) to PhD and other postdoctoral fellowships, with some dance scholars taking up their studies as *mature students* after a professional dance career.

Dance competitions

A **dance competition** is an organized event in which contestants perform dances before a judge or judges for awards and, in some cases, monetary prizes. There are several major types of dance competitions, distinguished primarily by the style or styles of dances performed. Major types of dance competitions include:

- **Competitive dance**, in which a variety of theater dance styles—such as acro, ballet, jazz, hip-hop, lyrical, and tap—are permitted.
- **Open** competitions, which permit a wide variety of dance styles. A popular example of this is the TV program So You Think You Can Dance.

Morris dancing in the grounds of Wells Cathedral, Wells, England

An amateur dancesport competition at MIT

Professional dancers at the Tropicana Club, Havana, Cuba, in 2008

- **Dancesport**, which is focused exclusively on ballroom and latin dance. Popular examples of this are TV programs Dancing with the Stars and Strictly Come Dancing.
- **Single-style** competitions, such as highland dance, dance team, and Irish dance, which only permit a single dance style.

Today, there are various dances and dance show competitions on Television and the Internet.

Dance occupations

There are different careers connected with dancing: Dancer, dance teacher, dance sport coach, dance therapist and choreographer.

Dancer

Dance training differs depending on the dance form. There are university programs and schools associated with professional dance companies for specialised training in classical dance (e.g. Ballet) and modern dance. There are also smaller, privately owned dance studios where students may train in a variety of dance forms including competitive dance forms (e.g. Latin dance, ballroom dance, etc.) as well as ethnic/traditional dance forms.

Professional dancers are usually employed on contract or for particular performances/productions. The professional life of a dancer is generally one of constantly changing work situations, strong competition pressure and low pay. Professional dancers often need to supplement their income, either in dance related roles (e.g., dance teaching, dance sport coaches, yoga) or Pilates instruction to achieve financial stability.

In the U.S. many professional dancers are members of unions such as the American Guild of Musical Artists, the Screen Actors Guild and Actors' Equity Association. The unions help determine working conditions and minimum salaries for their members.

Dance teachers

Dance teacher and operators of dance schools rely on reputation and marketing. For dance forms without an association structure such as Salsa or Tango Argentino they may not have formal training. Most dance teachers are self employed.

Dancesport coaches

Dancesport coaches are tournament dancers or former dancesports people, and may be recognised by a dance sport federation.

Choreographer

Choreographers are generally university trained and are typically employed for particular projects or, more rarely may work on contract as the resident choreographer for a specific dance company. A choreographic work is protected intellectual property. Dancers may undertake their own choreography.

Dance by ethnicity or region

Main article: List of ethnic, regional, and folk dances sorted by origin

India

Main article: Dance in India

During the first millennium BCE in India, many texts were composed which attempted to codify aspects of daily life. In the matter of dance, Bharata Muni's *Natyashastra* (literally *"the text of dramaturgy"*) is the one of the earlier texts. Though the main theme of *Natyashastra* deals with drama, dance is also widely featured, and indeed the two concepts have ever since been linked in Indian culture. The text elaborates various hand-gestures or mudras and classifies movements of the various limbs of the body, gait, and so on. The Natyashastra categorised dance into four groups and into four regional varieties, naming the groups: secular, ritual, abstract, and, interpretive. However, concepts of regional geography has altered and so have regional varieties of Indian dances. Dances like *"Odra Magadhi"*, which after decades long debate, has been traced to present day Mithila-Orissa region's dance form of Odissi, indicate influence of dances in cultural interactions between different regions.

From these beginnings rose the various classical styles which are recognised today. Therefore, all Indian classical dances are to varying degrees rooted in the Natyashastra and therefore share common features: for example, the mudras, some body positions, and the inclusion of dramatic or expressive acting or abhinaya. The Indian classical music tradition provides the accompaniment for the dance, and as percussion is such an integral part of the tradition, the dancers of nearly all the styles wear bells around their ankles to counterpoint and complement the percussion.

Bhangra in the Punjab

Main article: Bhangra

The Punjab area overlapping India and Pakistan is the place of origin of Bhangra. It is widely known both as a style of music and a dance. It is mostly related to ancient harvest celebrations, love, patriotism or social issues. Its music is coordinated by a musical instrument called the 'Dhol'. Bhangra is not just music but a dance, a celebration of the harvest where people beat the dhol (drum), sing Boliyaan (lyrics) and dance.It developed further with the Vaisakhi festival of the Sikhs.

Dances of Sri Lanka

Main article: Dances of Sri Lanka

The devil dances of Sri Lanka or "yakun natima" are a carefully crafted ritual with a history reaching far back into Sri Lanka's pre-Buddhist past. It combines ancient "Ayurvedic" concepts of disease causation with psychological manipulation. The dance combines many aspects including Sinhalese cosmology, the dances also has an impact on the classical dances of Sri Lanka.

In Europe and North America

Concert (or performance) dance

Main article: Concert dance

Ballet

Main article: Ballet

Harlequin and Columbine from the mime theater at *Tivoli* , Denmark

Ballet developed first in Italy and then in France from lavish court spectacles that combined music, drama, poetry, song, costumes and dance. Members of the court nobility took part as performers. During the reign of Louis XIV, himself a dancer, dance became more codified. Professional dancers began to take the place of court amateurs, and ballet masters were licensed by the French government. The first ballet dance academy was the Académie Royale de Danse (Royal Dance Academy), opened in Paris in 1661. Shortly thereafter, the first institutionalized ballet troupe, associated with the Academy, was formed; this troupe began as an all-male ensemble but by 1681 opened to include women as well.

20th century concert dance

Main article: 20th century concert dance

At the beginning of the 20th century, there was an explosion of innovation in dance style characterized by an exploration of freer technique. Early pioneers of what became known as modern dance include Loie Fuller, Isadora Duncan, Mary Wigman and Ruth St. Denis. The relationship of music to dance serves as the basis for Eurhythmics, devised by Emile Jaques-Dalcroze, which was influential to the development of Modern dance and modern ballet through artists such

A small dance company rehearses for an outdoor performance in Stuyvesant Cove Park in Manhattan, New York City

as Marie Rambert. Eurythmy, developed by Rudolf Steiner and Marie Steiner-von Sivers, combines formal elements reminiscent of traditional dance with the new freer style, and introduced a complex new vocabulary to dance. In the 1920s, important founders of the new style such as Martha Graham and Doris Humphrey began their work. Since this time, a wide variety of dance styles have been developed; see Modern dance.

The influence of African American dance

Main article: African American dance

African American dances are those dances which have developed within African American communities in everyday spaces, rather than in dance studios, schools or companies and its derivatives, tap dance, disco, jazz dance, swing dance, hip hop dance and breakdance. Other dances, such as the lindy hop with its relationship to rock and roll music and rock and roll dance have also had a global influence.

Performing arts
Major forms
Dance · Music · Opera · Theatre · Circus
Minor forms
Magic · Puppetry
Genres
Drama · Tragedy · Comedy · Tragicomedy · Romance · Satire · Epic · Lyric

See also

Main articles: Outline of dance and Index of dance articles

- African American dance
- *An American Ballroom Companion*
- Backup dancer
- Ballroom dance
- Cheerleading
- Entrainment (Biomusicology)
- Feather Award
- Health risks of professional dance
- Dance costumes
- Dance criticism
- Dance theory
- Majorettes

- List of choreographers
- List of dance style categories
- List of dance topics
- List of dance wikibooks

References

Notes

Further reading

- Adshead-Lansdale, J. (Ed.) (1994) *Dance History: An Introduction*. Routledge. ISBN 0-415-09030-X.
- Carter, A. (1998) *The Routledge Dance Studies Reader*. Routledge. ISBN 0-415-16447-8.
- Charman, S. Kraus, R, G. Chapman, S. and Dixon-Stowall, B. (1990) *History of the Dance in Art and Education*. Pearson Education. ISBN 0-13-389362-6.
- Cohen, S, J. (1992) *Dance As a Theatre Art: Source Readings in Dance History from 1581 to the Present*. Princeton Book Co. ISBN 0-87127-173-7.
- Daly, A. (2002) *Critical Gestures: Writings on Dance and Culture*. Wesleyan University Press. ISBN 0-8195-6566-0.
- Dils, A. (2001) *Moving History/Dancing Cultures: A Dance History Reader*. Wesleyan University Press. ISBN 0-8195-6413-3.
- Miller, James, L. (1986) *Measures of Wisdom: The Cosmic Dance in Classical and Christian Antiquity*, University of Toronto Press. ISBN 0802025536.

External links

- Chisholm, Hugh, ed (1911). "Dance". *Encyclopædia Britannica* (Eleventh ed.). Cambridge University Press.

- Historic illustrations of dancing from 3300 B.C. to 1911 A.D. [1] from Project Gutenberg
- United States National Museum of Dance and Hall of Fame [2]

pnb:چان ckb:□□□پ□کر□

Reasons to Party

Saint Patrick's Day

Saint Patrick's Day	
The Chicago River is dyed green each year for the St. Patrick's Day celebration, shown here in 2009.	
Also called	St Patrick's Day St Paddy's Day Patrick's Day Paddy's Day
Observed by	Irish people and people of Irish ancestry, non-Irish celebrants
Type	National, Ethnic, Catholic
Date	March 17
Observances	Attending mass or service, attending parades, attending céilithe, wearing shamrocks, wearing green

Saint Patrick's Day (Irish: *Lá Fhéile Pádraig*) is a yearly holiday celebrated on the 17th of March. It is named after Saint Patrick (*circa* AD 387–461), the most commonly recognised of the patron saints of Ireland. It began as a purely Catholic holiday and became an official feast day in the early 17th century. It has gradually become more of a secular celebration of Ireland's culture.

It is a public holiday in the Republic of Ireland and a large, national multi day festival now takes place each year called St. Patrick's Festival. In Northern Ireland it is a bank holiday instead. The Northern Ireland Assembly has discussed this frequently but as of yet no decision has been made to make it a public holiday. It is a public holiday in Newfoundland and Labrador and in Montserrat. It is also widely celebrated by the Irish diaspora, especially in places such as Great Britain, Canada, the United States, Argentina, Australia, New Zealand, and Montserrat, among others.

Saint Patrick

Main article: Saint Patrick

Little is known of Patrick's early life, though it is known that he was born in Roman Britain in the 4th century, into a wealthy Romano-British family. His father and grandfather were deacons in the Church. At the age of sixteen, he was kidnapped by Irish raiders and taken captive to Ireland as a slave. It is believed he was held somewhere on the west coast of Ireland, possibly Mayo, but the exact location is unknown. According to his Confession, he was told by God in a dream to flee from captivity to the coast, where he would board a ship and return to Britain. Upon returning, he quickly joined the Church in Auxerre in Gaul and studied to be a priest.[citation needed]

Saint Patrick (c. 387–461)

In 432, he again said that he was called back to Ireland, though as a bishop, to Christianize the Irish from their native polytheism. Irish folklore tells that one of his teaching methods included using the shamrock to explain the Christian doctrine of the Trinity to the Irish people. After nearly thirty years of evangelism, he died on 17 March 461, and according to tradition, was buried at Downpatrick. Although there were other more successful missions to Ireland from Rome, Patrick endured as the principal champion of Irish Christianity and is held in esteem in the Irish Church.

Wearing of the green

Originally, the colour associated with Saint Patrick was blue. Over the years the colour green and its association with Saint Patrick's day grew. Green ribbons and shamrocks were worn in celebration of St Patrick's Day as early as the 17th century. He is said to have used the shamrock, a three-leaved plant, to explain the Holy Trinity to the pagan Irish, and the wearing and display of shamrocks and shamrock-inspired designs have become a ubiquitous feature of the day. In the 1798 rebellion, in hopes of making a political statement, Irish soldiers wore full green uniforms on 17 March in hopes of catching public attention. The phrase "the wearing of the green", meaning to wear a shamrock on one's clothing, derives from a song of the same name.

Outside Ireland

In Argentina

In Argentina, and especially in Buenos Aires, all-night long parties are celebrated in designated streets, since the weather is comfortably warm in March. People dance and drink only beer throughout the night, until seven or eight in the morning, and although the tradition of mocking those who do not wear green does not exist, many people wear something green. In Buenos Aires, the party is held in the downtown street of Reconquista, where there are several Irish pubs; in 2006, there were 50,000 people in this street and the pubs nearby. Neither the Catholic Church nor the Irish community, the fifth largest in the world outside Ireland, take part in the organization of the parties.

In Canada

The longest-running Saint Patrick's Day parade in Canada occurs each year in Montreal, the flag of which has a shamrock in one of its corners. The parades have been held in continuity since 1824.<ref name="St. Patrick's Day Parades In the province of Manitoba, the Irish Association of Manitoba runs an annual three day festival of music and culture based around St Patrick's Day.[citation needed]

Saint Patrick's Day celebrations in Montreal

Saint Patrick's Day Parade in Montreal

In 2004, the CelticFest Vancouver Society organized an annual festival in downtown Vancouver to celebrate the Celtic Nations and their culture. This event, which includes a parade, occurs the weekend closest to Saint Patrick's Day.

The Toronto Maple Leafs hockey team was known as the Toronto St. Patricks from 1919 to 1927, and wore green jerseys. In 1999, when the Maple Leafs played on *Hockey Night in Canada* (national broadcast of the NHL) on Saint Patrick's Day, they wore the green St. Patrick's day-themed retro uniforms. There is a large parade in the city's downtown core that attracts over 100,000 spectators.[citation needed]

Some groups, notably Guinness, have lobbied to make Saint Patrick's Day a national holiday in Canada. Currently, the Canadian province of Newfoundland and Labrador is the only jurisdiction in Canada where Saint Patrick's Day is a provincial holiday.

In March 2009, the Calgary Tower had changed its top exterior lights to new green-coloured CFL bulbs just in time for Saint Patrick's Day. The lights were in fact part of the environmental non-profit organization, Project Porchlight, and were Green to represent environmental concerns. Approximately 210 lights were changed in time for Saint Patrick's Day and almost resemble a Leprechaun's hat during the evening light. After a week, regular white CFLs took their place, saving the Calgary Tower around $12,000 and reducing greenhouse gas emissions by 104 metric tonnes in the process.

In Great Britain

In Great Britain, the Queen Mother used to present bowls of shamrock flown over from Ireland to members of the Irish Guards, a regiment in the British Army consisting primarily of soldiers from both Northern Ireland and the Republic of Ireland. The Irish Guards still wear shamrock on this day, flown in from Ireland.

2006 St Patrick's Day celebrations in Trafalgar Square London

Horse racing at the Cheltenham Festival attracts large numbers of Irish people, both residents of Britain and many who travel from Ireland, and usually coincides with Saint Patrick's Day.

Birmingham holds the largest Saint Patrick's Day parade in Britain with a massive city centre parade over a two mile (3 km) route through the city centre. The organisers describe it as the third biggest parade in the world after Dublin and New York.

London, since 2002, has had an annual Saint Patrick's Day parade which takes place on weekends around the 17th, usually in Trafalgar Square. In 2008 the water in the Trafalgar Square fountains was dyed green.

Liverpool, a major port leading to the Irish Sea, has the highest proportion of residents of Irish ancestry of any English city.[citation needed] This has led to a long-standing celebration on St Patrick's Day in terms of music, cultural events and the parade.

Manchester hosts a two-week Irish festival in the weeks prior to St Patrick's Day. The festival includes an Irish Market based at the city's town hall which flies the Irish tricolour opposite the Union Flag, a large parade as well as a large number of cultural and learning events throughout the two-week period.

.

The Scottish town of Coatbridge, where the majority of the town's population are of Irish descent,[citation needed] also has a St. Patrick's Day Festival which includes celebrations and parades in the town centre.

Glasgow began an annual Saint Patrick's Day parade and festival in 2007.

In Montserrat

The tiny island of Montserrat, known as "Emerald Island of the Caribbean" because of its founding by Irish refugees from Saint Kitts and Nevis, is the only place in the world apart from Ireland and the Canadian province of Newfoundland and Labrador where St Patrick's Day is a public holiday. The holiday commemorates a failed slave uprising that occurred on 17 March 1798.

In South Korea

Seoul(Capital city of South Korea) have celebrated Saint Patrick's Day since 2001 with Irish Association of Korea. The place of parade and festival has been moved from Itaewon and Daehangno to Cheonggyecheon.

In New Zealand

Saint Patrick's Day is widely celebrated in New Zealand - green items of clothing are traditionally worn and the streets are often filled with revellers drinking and making merry from early afternoon until late at night.

The Irish made a large impact in New Zealand's social, political and education systems, owing to the large numbers that emigrated there during the 19th century and Saint Patrick's Day is seen as a day to celebrate individual links to Ireland and Irish heritage.

In Japan

Saint Patrick's Parades are now held in 9 locations across Japan. The first parade, in Tokyo, was organized by The Irish Network Japan (INJ) in 1992. Nowadays Parades and other events related to Saint Patrick's Day spread across almost the entire month of March. It gets quite busy.

In the United States

Early celebrations

Irish Society of Boston organized what was not only the first Saint Patrick's Day Parade in the colonies but the first recorded Saint Patrick's Day Parade in the world on 18 March 1737.Wikipedia:Identifying reliable sources (The first parade in Ireland did not occur until 1931 in Dublin.) This parade in Boston involved Irish immigrant workers marching to make a political statement about how they were not happy with their

The north White House fountain was dyed green in celebration of Saint Patrick's Day in 2009 and 2010.

low social status and their inability to obtain jobs in America. New York's first Saint Patrick's Day Parade was held on 17 March 1762 by Irish soldiers in the British Army.The first celebration of Saint Patrick's Day in New York City was held at the Crown and Thistle Tavern in 1766, the parades were held as political and social statements because the Irish immigrants were being treated unfairly. In 1780, General George Washington, who commanded soldiers of Irish descent in the Continental Army, allowed his troops a holiday on 17 March "as an act of solidarity with the Irish in their fight for independence." This event became known as The St. Patrick's Day Encampment of 1780. Wikipedia:Identifying reliable sources

Irish patriotism in New York City continued to soar and the parade in New York City continued to grow. Irish aid societies were created like Friendly Sons of St. Patrick and the Hibernian Society and they marched in the parades too. Finally when many of these aid societies joined forces in 1848 the parade became not only the largest parade in the United States but one of the largest in the world.

Postcard postmarked 1912 in the United States

Customs today

In every year since 1991, March has been proclaimed Irish-American Heritage Month by the US Congress or President due to the date of St. Patrick's Day. Today, Saint Patrick's Day is widely celebrated in America by Irish and non-Irish alike. It is one of the leading days for consumption of alcohol in the United States, and is typically one of the busiest days of the year for bars and restaurants. Many people, regardless of ethnic background, wear green clothing and items. Traditionally, those who are caught not wearing green are pinched affectionately.

Seattle and other cities paint the traffic stripe of their parade routes green. Chicago dyes its river green and has done so since 1962 when sewer workers used green dye to check for sewer discharges and had the idea to turn the river green for Saint Patrick's Day. Originally 100 pounds of vegetable dye was used to turn the river green for a whole week but now only forty pounds of dye is used and the colour only lasts for several hours. Indianapolis also dyes its main canal green. Savannah dyes its downtown city fountains green. Missouri University of Science and Technology - St Pat's Board Alumni paint 12 city blocks kelly green with mops before the annual parade.[citation needed] In Jamestown, New York, the Chadakoin River (a small tributary that connects Conewango Creek with its source at Chautauqua Lake) is dyed green each year.

Columbia, SC dyes its fountain green in the area known as Five Points (a popular collegiate location near the University of South Carolina). A two day celebration is held over St Patrick's Day weekend. In

Boston, Evacuation Day is celebrated as a public holiday for Suffolk County. While officially commemorating the British departure from Boston, it was made an official holiday after Saint Patrick's Day parades had been occurring in Boston for several decades, and is often believed to have been popularized because of its falling on the same day as Saint Patrick's Day.

In the Northeastern United States, peas are traditionally planted on Saint Patrick's Day.

Parades

Many parades are held to celebrate the holiday. The longest-running of these are:

- Boston, Massachusetts, since 1737
- New York City, since 1762
- Philadelphia, Pennsylvania, since 1771
- Morristown, New Jersey, since 1780
- New Orleans, Louisiana, since 1809
- Buffalo, New York, since 1811
- Savannah, Georgia, since 1813
- Carbondale, Pennsylvania, since 1833
- New Haven, Connecticut, since 1842
- Milwaukee, Wisconsin, since 1843
- Chicago, Illinois, since 1843
- Saint Paul, Minnesota, since 1851
- San Francisco, California, since 1852
- Scranton, Pennsylvania, since 1862
- Cleveland, Ohio, since 1867
- Pittsburgh, Pennsylvania, since 1869
- Kansas City, Missouri, since 1873
- Butte, Montana, since 1882

Saint Patrick's Day parade, San Francisco, 2007.

St. Patricks day parade in Grand Ledge, Michigan, 2008.

- Rolla, Missouri, since 1909

U.S. cities with major celebrations

Buffalo, New York

The city of Buffalo has two Saint Patrick's Day parades. The first is the "Old Neighborhood Parade," which is in its 17th year in 2010 and takes place in the city's historic Old First Ward in South Buffalo on the Saturday before Saint Patrick's Day. The older, larger "Buffalo St. Patrick's Day Parade" (in its 68th consecutive year in 2010) also takes place, usually on the Sunday before Saint Patrick's Day. That parade runs from Niagara Square along Delaware Avenue to North Street. The Buffalo parade is the 3rd largest parade in New York State behind the New York City Parade and the Pearl River Parade.

Butte, Montana

Butte's mixed heritage and mining history brought in a large population of Irish immigrants. The yearly event brings in visitors from all over the world and doubles the city's population for the day. Butte has a long history of running a parade and concerts in the uptown area. There currently is not an open container law in Butte Montana and the event often becomes rowdy.

Dallas, Texas

Each year since 1981 a parade and after party has been held on Lower Greenville Avenue. The parade is held the Saturday before St. Patricks day with thousands of spectators and partiers lining the streets. It is the biggest St. Patrick's Day parade and festival in the Southwest. There is also a run before the parade on Greenville.

Hoboken, New Jersey

The New Jersey town of Hoboken has held an annual St. Patricks Day parade since 1986. The parade takes place at 1 PM and marches down Washington Street from 14th Street to 1st Street.

Over the years, there has been much controversy surrounding the public intoxication during this event. The city has issued a zero tolerance policy, and has been inacting $2,000 minimum fines for any alcohol related offence.

Holyoke, Massachusetts

This Western Mass factory town was the site of massive Irish immigration in the 19th Century, and hosts a Parade its organizers claim is the second largest in the United States. It is scheduled on the Sunday following Saint Patrick's Day each year. Attendance exceeds 300,000, with over 25,000 marchers, through a 2.3-mile route in this city of 40,000. A 10K road Race and many events create a remarkable festival weekend. Each year an Irish-American who has distinguished himself or herself in their chosen profession is awarded the John F. Kennedy National Award. JFK was a National Award Winner in the 1958 Holyoke Parade. Other winners include author Tom Clancy, Homeland Security Director Tom Ridge, and actor Pat O'Brien

Hot Springs, Arkansas

The Hot Springs, Arkansas parade is among world's Shortest St. Patrick's Day Parade, held annually on historic Bridge Street, designated "The Shortest Street in the World" in the 1940s by Ripley's Believe It or Not.

Las Vegas, Nevada

The Southern Nevada, (formerly Las Vegas) Sons of Erin have put on a parade since 1966. It was formerly held on Fremont Street in downtown Las Vegas, later moved to 4th street. Since 2005, the parade has been held in downtown Henderson. It is one of the biggest parades in the state of Nevada. It also consists of a three day festival, carnival and classic car show in Old Town Henderson.

New Orleans

Historically the largest entry port for Irish immigrants in the U.S. South, New Orleans has maintained a large population of Irish heritage, and Saint Patrick's Day traditions going back to the 19th century, including multiple block parties and parades.

Revelers vie for a tossed cabbage, New Orleans

The New Orleans parades are mostly based around neighborhood and community organizations. Major parades include the Irish Channel parade, the Downtown Irish Parade starting in the Bywater neighborhood, multiple parades in the French Quarter, and a combined Irish-Italian Parade celebrating both Saint Patrick's Day and Saint Joseph's Day.

As with many parades in New Orleans, the influence of New Orleans Mardi Gras is apparent, with some of the floats being reused from local Carnival parades, and beads and trinkets being thrown to those along the parade route. New Orleans Saint Patrick's Day parades are also famous for throwing onions, carrots, cabbages, potatoes, and other ingredients for making an Irish stew.

Various suburbs and surrounding communities also hold celebrations, including parades in Metairie, Slidell, and an Irish Italian Isleño Parade in Chalmette.

New York City

The New York parade has not only become the largest Saint Patrick's Day parade in the world but it is also the oldest civilian parade in the world. In a typical year, 150,000 marchers participate in it, including bands, firefighters, military and police groups, county associations, emigrant societies, and social and cultural clubs, and 2 million spectators line the streets. The parade marches up the 1.5 mile route along 5th Avenue in Manhattan, is a five hour procession, and is always led by the U.S. 69th Infantry Regiment. The Commissioner of the parade always asks the Commanding Officer if the 69th is ready, to which the

Saint Patrick's Parade on Fifth Avenue, 1909

response is, "The 69th is always ready." New York politicians - or those running for office - are always found prominently marching in the parade. Former New York City Mayor Ed Koch once proclaimed himself "Ed O'Koch" for the day, and he continued to don an Irish sweater and march every year up until 2003, even though he was no longer in office.

The parade is organized and run by the Ancient Order of Hibernians.[citation needed] For many years, the Saint Patrick's Day Parade was the primary public function of the organization. On occasion the order has appointed controversial Irish republican figures (some of whom were barred from the U.S.) to be its Grand Marshal.[citation needed] The parade has also drawn controversy for many years for its exclusion of openly gay organizations. In 1989 Dorothy Hayden Cudahy became the first female Grand Marshal of the St. Patrick's Day Parade; in 1984 she had become the first woman, as well as the first American-born person, to be elected president of the County Kilkenny Association [1] [2].

The New York parade is moved to the previous Saturday (16 March) in years where 17 March is a Sunday. The event also has been moved on the rare occasions when, due to Easter falling on a very early date, 17 March would land in Holy Week. This same scenario arose again in 2008, when Easter fell on March 23, but the festivities went ahead on their normal date and received record viewers. In many other American cities (such as San Francisco), the parade is always

Saint Patrick's Day celebration, Union Army. Irish Brigade holds a steeplechase race, March 17, 1863.

held on the Sunday before 17 March, regardless of the liturgical calendar.

Pearl River, New York

Pearl River attracts a crowd of 100,000 people, making it the second largest parade in New York state behind the New York City Parade. The parade started in 1963.,

Rolla, Missouri

Rolla is home to the Missouri University of Science & Technology (formerly known as University of Missouri-Rolla, and Missouri School of Mines), an engineering college. Saint Patrick is the patron saint of engineers, the school and town's celebrations start ten days before Saint Patrick's Day, with a downtown parade held the Saturday before Saint Patrick's. A royal court is crowned, and the streets in the city's downtown area are painted solid green. Each year's celebrations are said to be "The Best Ever." In 2008, Rolla celebrated its "100th Annual Best Ever St. Patrick's Day 2008" celebration.

In previous years, a pit of green liquid was made by students as part of the festivities, and named 'Alice' -- stepping into Alice was a rite of bravery. In recent years the university faculty has banned the practice out of health concerns.

Savannah, Georgia

The parade organizers have claimed an expected attendance of around 400,000. In 2006, the Tánaiste was featured in the parade. The parade travels through Savannah's Historic District. One tradition that has developed has been the official "dyeing of the fountains" which happens several days before the parade.

Scranton, Pennsylvania

Due to the rich history of Scranton participation in Saint Patrick's Day festivities it is one of the oldest and most populated parades in the United States. It has been going on annually since 1862 by the St. Patrick's Day Parade Association of Lackawanna County and the parade has gotten attention nationally as being one of the better Saint Patrick's Day parades. The parade route begins on Wyoming Ave. and loops up to Penn Ave. and then Lackawanna Ave. before going back down over Jefferson Ave. to get to Washington Ave. Scranton hosts the third largest Saint Patrick's Day Parade in the United States. In 2008, up to 150,000 people attended the parade.

Seattle, Washington

Seattle Washington's Saint Patrick's Day Parade, recognized by CNN in 2009 as one of the "Five places to get your green on" in America, travels along a 1-mile route through the Emerald City's downtown financial and retail core the Saturday before Saint Patrick's Day. Seattle's Saint Patrick's Day Celebration is the largest and oldest in the Northwestern United States. In 2009, some 20,000 spectators and groups from throughout the Northwest turned out for the city's Irish

Seattle's Festál Irish Festival

shenanigans. Along with the annual "Laying 'O the Green" where Irish revellers mark the path of the next morning's procession with a mile-long green stripe, the Seattle parade marks the high-point of Seattle's Irish Week festivities. The week-long civic celebration organized by the city's Irish Heritage Club [3] includes the annual Society of the Friends of St. Patrick Dinner where a century-old Irish Shillelagh has been passed to the group's new president for 70 years, an Irish Soda Bread Baking Contest, a Mass for Peace that brings together Catholics and others in a Protestant church, and the annual Irish Week Festival, which takes place around Saint Patrick's Day is enormous, including step dancing, food, historical and modern exhibitions, and Irish lessons. Many celebrities of Irish descent visit Seattle during it's Saint Patrick's Day Celebration. In 2010 The Right Honourable Desmond Guinness, a direct descendant of Guinness Brewery founder Arthur Guinness, will serve as the parade's grand marshal. In 2009, The Tonight Show's Conan O'Brien made a guest appearance at the annual Mayor's Proclamation Luncheon at local Irish haunt F.X. McCrory's. And in 2008, European Union Ambassador to the U.S. and former Irish Prime Minister John Bruton served as the parade's grand marshal and marched alongside Tom Costello, the mayor of Galway, Seattle's Irish sister city. There is also another Saint Patrick's Day Parade,that also takes place in Washington's eastern side of the state in Spokane.

Syracuse, New York

In the city of Syracuse, NY, Saint Patrick's celebrations are traditionally begun with the delivery of green beer to Coleman's Irish Pub on the first Sunday of March. Coleman's is located in the Tipperary Hill section of the city. Tipperary Hill is home to the World famous "Green-on-Top" Traffic Light and is historically the Irish section in Syracuse. Saint Patrick's Day is rung in at midnight with the painting of a Shamrock under the Green-Over-Red traffic light. Syracuse boasts the largest Saint Patrick's Day celebration per-capita in the United States with their annual Syracuse Saint Patrick's Parade, founded by Nancy Duffy, an honoured journalist in the Central New York area and an active community leader, and Daniel F. Casey, a local Irishman and businessman. "The parade remains a major annual event, typically drawing an estimated crowd of more than 100,000 visitors to downtown Syracuse, as well as 5,000 to 6,000 marchers."

Tallahassee, Florida

The Tallahassee Irish Society [4] has been hosting an annual St. Patricks day event in Tallahassee since 1999. In 2010, along with the City of Tallahassee, the first annual St. Patricks Day parade and Downtown Get Down is being hosted along Adams Street.

Sports-related celebrations

Baseball

Although Major League Baseball is still in its preseason spring training phase when Saint Patrick's Day rolls around, some teams celebrate by wearing holiday-themed uniforms. The Cincinnati Reds were the first team to ever wear Saint Patrick's Day hats in 1978. The Boston Red Sox were the second team to start wearing Saint Patrick's Day hats in 1990. Many teams have since started wearing St. Patrick's day themed jerseys, including the Philadelphia Phillies in the 1980s and Boston Red Sox in 2004. Since then it has become a tradition of many sports teams to also wear special uniforms to celebrate the holiday. The Los Angeles Dodgers also have a history with the Irish-American community. With the O'Malley family owning the team and now Frank McCourt, the Dodgers have had team celebrations or worn green jerseys on Saint Patrick's Day. The Detroit Tigers and Philadelphia Phillies also wear St. Patrick's Day caps and jerseys. Other teams celebrate by wearing kelly green hats. These teams include: the Chicago Cubs, the Chicago White Sox, the New York Mets, the San Diego Padres, the Atlanta Braves, the Pittsburgh Pirates, the Kansas City Royals, the Seattle Mariners and the St. Louis Cardinals. The Washington Nationals have fan green hat day on September 17 to represent 6 months to Saint Patrick's Day.

Nearly all MLB teams now produce Saint Patrick's Day merchandise, including Kelly green hats, jerseys, and t-shirts.

Basketball

Between 15 and 17 March 2009, a number of NBA teams wore green jerseys in recognition of Saint Patrick's Day including the New York Knicks, Chicago Bulls, Toronto Raptors and Dallas Mavericks. The Boston Celtics, whose road jersey is green, wore a specially designed green and gold jersey.

Ice hockey

While no NHL teams currently don green jerseys during Saint Patrick's Day games, the league has offered a line of holiday-themed gear to its fans in recent years.

Gaelic Games

Traditionally the All-Ireland Senior Club Football Championship and All-Ireland Senior Club Hurling Championship are held on Saint Patrick's Day in Croke Park, Dublin. The Interprovincial Championship was previously held on March 17 but this was switched to games being played in Autumn.

Rugby Union

The Leinster Schools Rugby Senior Cup, Munster Schools Rugby Senior Cup and Ulster Schools Senior Cup are held on Saint Patricks Day. The Connacht Schools Rugby Senior Cup is held on the weekend before Saint Patrick's Day.

See also

- Irish calendar
- It's a Great Day for the Irish
- Plastic Paddy
- Public holidays in the Republic of Ireland
- Public holidays in the United Kingdom

External links

- The Life, Miracles and Prayers of St. Patrick of Ireland, Patron Saint of Ireland [5]
- Official St. Patrick's Festival in Dublin, Ireland [6]
- Saint Patrick History [7]
- Two books on St. Patrick [8]
- St. Patrick's Day History [9] - slideshow by *The Huffington Post*
- St. Patrick's Day [10] on The History Channel

New Year's Eve

New Year's Eve	
Also called	Hogmanay (Scotland), Calennig (Wales), Silvester (Austria, Croatia, Czech Republic, France, Germany, Hungary, Israel, Italy, Poland, Slovakia, Slovenia, Ukraine), Réveillon (France), Ano Novo (Brazil, Portugal), Año Nuevo (Argentina), Nochevieja (Spain, Hispanic America) Oud en Nieuw (Netherlands, Belgium, Suriname, Netherlands Antilles)
Observed by	People around the world
Type	International
Significance	The final day of the Gregorian year
Date	31 December, climaxing at midnight
Celebrations	Reflections, Late-Night Partying, Family- Gatherings, Feasting, Present Exchanges, Fireworks, Countdowns
Related to	New Year's Day

New Year's Eve or **Old Year's Night** is on 31 December, the final day of the Gregorian year, and the day before New Year's Day.

New Year's Eve is a separate observance from the observance of New Year's Day. In modern Western practice, New Year's Eve is celebrated with parties and social gatherings spanning the transition of the year at midnight.

Many cultures use fireworks and other forms of noise making in part of the celebration. New Year's Eve is observed universally on 31 December according to the year numbering of the Common Era, or A.D. Anno Domini convention, even in non-Christian nations. New Year's Eve is also the seventh day of Christmas in western Christianity. Traditional and religious celebrations for e.g. the Chinese, Muslim and Jewish new year, which occur on different dates, are still celebrated separately in the cultures that observe them, on the appropriate dates each year.

Localised celebrations

Australia

Each major city around Australia holds New Year's Eve celebrations, usually accompanied by a fireworks display amongst other events. Gloucester Park, a racecourse in central Perth, is the largest and most recognised display in Perth. In Brisbane 50,000 people annually gather at sites around the Brisbane River in the city to watch a fireworks display while events are held in the city and at Southbank.

Fireworks at Sydney Harbour.

The two largest New Year's Eve celebrations in Australia are held in its two largest cities, Sydney and Melbourne. The celebrations in Sydney are usually accompanied by a theme which is displayed in light shows and a large symbol in the middle of the Sydney Harbour Bridge. Over 1.5 million people gathered around Port Jackson (Sydney attendance of 2 million people). The fireworks display last from 12 to 25 minutes and is followed by music shows set on several stages throughout the beach.

The Melbourne fireworks display as seen from Alexandra Gardens.

As one of the first major New Year's celebrations each year (due to time zones), Sydney's fireworks display is often broadcast throughout the world during the day of 31 December.

Austria

In Austria, the New Year's Eve is usually celebrated with friends and family. At exactly midnight, all radio and television programmes operated by ORF broadcast the sound of the Pummerin (bell of St Stephen's Cathedral in Vienna), and right after that the "Donauwalzer" (The Blue Danube) by Johann Strauss II is played, which many people dance to at parties or on the street. Large crowds gather on the streets of Vienna, where the municipal government organises a series of stages from which bands and orchestras play music. Fireworks are set off both by ordinary people and the municipal governments.

Belgium

Belgian New Year's Eve celebrations are held in all large cities on 1 January. These celebrations are usually accompanied by fireworks.

Brazil

The *Ano Novo* (*New Year* in Portuguese) celebration, also know in Brazilian Portuguese by the French word Reveillon, is one of the country's main holidays, and officially marks the beginning of the summer holidays, that usually end by Carnival (analogous to Memorial Day and Labor Day in the United States).

The beach of Copacabana (in Portuguese: *Praia de Copacabana*) is considered by many to be the location of the best fireworks show in the world. Brazilians usually have a copious meal with family or friends at home, in restaurants or private clubs, and consume alcoholic beverages. They usually dress in white, to bring good luck into the new year. Fireworks, offerings to African-Brazilian deities, eating grapes or lentils are some of the customs associated with the holiday.

The city of São Paulo also has a famous worldwide event: the Saint Silvester Marathon (*Corrida de São Silvestre*), which traverses streets between Paulista Avenue and the downtown area. It is contested by athletes of many countries, including such Olympic stars as the Kenyan runner Paul Tergat, who won it five times.

"As it is said all the countries without exception celebrate the New Year's Eve and eventually the New year. this is an event that concerns everyone and it is obvious that it is well celebrated!All the countries of the world celebrate in its own manner and the more spectacular it is, the better it is for the eyes of other countries.

Also in Paulista Avenue is a great New Year's Eve, with large fires burning in the midnight. Famous singers in Brazil are in the party. In moving from 2008 to 2009, 1 million people attended the party.

Canada

In Canada, New Year's traditions and celebrations vary from region to region. Generally, New Year's Eve (also known as *New Year's Eve Day* or *Veille du Jour de l'An* in French) in Canada is a social holiday. In major metropolitan areas such as Toronto and Montreal, major celebrations with music and fireworks are often held at midnight. Other common New Year's Eve celebrations such as late-night partying are also major events in these cities and other places around Canada. In some areas, such as in rural Quebec, people ice fish and drink with their friends until the early hours of January 1.

On television, the sketch comedy troupe *Royal Canadian Air Farce* had been known for their New Year's Eve specials on CBC, which in addition before the start of their weekly television series, was one of their first forays into television after years on radio. Consequentially, the series finale of their television series was a New Year's Eve special on December 31, 2008, although due to their popularity, the CBC requested that they return for a New Year's Eve special for 2009.

China

In China, although the celebrations of the Lunar New Year are not until a few weeks into the new year, celebrations of the Gregorian New Year are still held in some areas. Celebrations with fireworks and rock concerts have taken place in Beijing's Solana Blue Harbor Shopping Park.

Denmark

The Danes usually celebrate New Year's Eve, or *nytårsaften* in Danish, with their families or, more commonly nowadays, with their close friends, with fireworks and champagne. The evening meal on New Year's Eve is often more exclusive, and often consists of three courses; traditional desserts include Marzipan ring cake (*Danish: kransekage, lit.: ring cake*). Danes often watch the Queen's New Year's Speech on television. The climax is when the clock on the Copenhagen City Hall reaches twelve, and the thousands of gathered people at the city square cheer and set off their fireworks. As in Germany the national television station. Traditionally people go around town and throw old dishes at their friends and families doors. The amount of broken cutlery heaped at a door is a measure of the popularity of the owner. DR1 broadcasts Dinner for One (*in Danish: 90 års fødselsdagen (lit.: The 90th birthday)*).

Ecuador

Ecuador celebrates a unique tradition on the last day of the year. Elaborate effigies, called Años Viejos (Old Years) are created to represent people and events from the past year. Often these include political characters or leaders that the creator of the effigy may have disagreed with. The dummies are made of straw, newspaper, and old clothes, with papier-mâché masks. Often they are also stuffed with fire crackers. At midnight the effigies are lit on fire to symbolize burning away of the past year and welcoming of the New Year. The origin of the tradition has its roots in pagan Roman and pre-Roman Spanish traditions still celebrated in Europe and which were brought to many countries of Latin-America in colonial times.

Other rituals are performed for the health, wealth, prosperity and protection. For example, traditionally each person eats twelve grapes before midnight, making a wish with each grape. Popularly, yellow underwear is said to attract positive energies for the New Year. Finally, walking around the block with one's suitcase will bring the person the journey of their dreams.

France

The French call New Year's Eve "*la Saint-Sylvestre*". It is usually celebrated with a feast called *le Réveillon de la Saint-Sylvestre*. This feast customarily includes special dishes like foie gras , seafood such as oysters and drinks like champagne. The celebration can be a simple, intimate dinner with friends and family or a much fancier ball (*une soirée dansante*).

On *le Jour de l'An* (New Year's Day), friends and family exchange New Year's resolutions kisses and wishes, the main ones being "Bonne Année", Bonheur, Sante, Amour, Argent ("Good Year", Happiness, Health, Love and Money). Some people eat desserts made of ice cream

The holiday period ends on January 6 (The Twelfth Night)for the Epiphany , or *Jour des Rois*. On this day, they celebrate the Wise Men, eating a traditional type of flat pastry cake, la *galette des rois*, most often two sheets of puff pastry, filled

New Year's Eve fireworks in Paris

with *frangipane* (almond paste). The cake contains a *fève*, small china character, that whoever finds becomes king or queen and get to wear a gold paper crown, then chose their partner. This tradition can last up to weeks.

Germany

Germans call New Year's Eve *Silvester* because 31 December is the feast day of Pope St. Sylvester. Since 1972, each New Year's Eve, several German television stations broadcast a short English (recorded by West German television in 1963) theatrical performance titled *Dinner for One*. A punch line from the comedy sketch, "same procedure as every year", has become a catch phrase in Germany. Every year Berlin hosts one of the largest New Year's Eve celebrations in all of Europe which is attended by over a million people. The focal point is the Brandenburg Gate and the fireworks at midnight centered around that location. Germans have a reputation of spending large amounts of money on firecrackers and fireworks. At midnight, Germans toast to the New Year with a glass of Sekt (German sparkling wine) or champagne. 'Bleigießen' is another German New Year's Eve custom, which involves telling fortunes by the shapes made by molten lead dropped into cold water.

Great Britain

Britain traditionally welcomes the new year with the chimes of Big Ben. Many cities have large firework displays and street parties, the two main events being in London and Edinburgh.

England

The main celebrations are broadcasted showing London's firework display, which is centred around the London Eye. It is one of the world's biggest fireworks displays for New Year. At the start of 2005, fireworks were launched from the wheel itself for the first time. The timing of the new year is usually indicated by the chimes on Big Ben.

The celebrations have been televised from London over the last few years by the BBC in England and Wales. Other major displays are held in Birmingham, Manchester, Liverpool, Leeds and Newcastle . Bideford in North Devon is also renowned for its New Year's Eve celebrations and traditional fancy dress, the centre of the celebrations on the quayside and around the Old Bridge.

Wales

Welsh celebrations on New Year's Eve are known as Calennig. The tradition of giving gifts and money on New Year's Day is an ancient custom that survives even in modern-day Wales, though nowadays it is now customary to give bread and cheese.

Thousands of people descend every year on Cardiff city centre to enjoy live music, catering, ice-skating, funfairs and fireworks. Many of the celebrations take place at Cardiff Castle and Cardiff City Hall.

Scotland

Scotland celebrates New Year as Hogmanay, and is celebrated greatly across the country with several different customs, such as First Footing, which involves friends or family members going to each others houses with a gift of whisky and sometimes a lump of coal. Other cities across Scotland, such as Aberdeen, Glasgow, and Stirling also have celebrations, also with fireworks at midnight.

Hogmanay Fireworks in Edinburgh

Edinburgh has one of the world's most famous New Year celebrations with the focus being a major street party along Princes Street. The cannon is fired at Edinburgh Castle at the stroke of midnight and is followed by a large fireworks display. Edinburgh, the Scottish capital, hosts a full 4 or 5 day festival stretching from the 28th to either New Year's Day or 2 January, which is also a Bank holiday in Scotland, unlike the rest of the United Kingdom.

BBC Scotland broadcast the celebrations in Edinburgh to a Scottish audience, with the celebrations also broadcast across the world. STV covers the New Year celebrations worldwide, with additionally providing coverage in Scotland of events going on around the country.

Guatemala

In the town of Antigua, Guatemala, people usually get together at the Santa Catalina Clock Arch to celebrate.

Guatemalans down a grape with each of the twelve chimes of the bell during the New Year countdown, while making a wish with each one.

Other traditions include sweeping the dirt out and taking luggage outside as a symbol of future trips.

The celebrations are very similar to those of Mexico and Spain.

Hong Kong

In Hong Kong, the people usually get together in Central, Causeway Bay and Tsim Sha Tsui to celebrate and to look at the night lights along the harbor. The Times Square shopping mall in Hong Kong also holds their own send-off to the ball drop held at Times Square in New York City.

Iceland

"Gleðilegt nýtt ár" is "Happy new year" in Icelandic. In Iceland the biggest new year events are usually in the greater Reykjavik area. Fireworks are very popular in Iceland. Bonfires are also set in several places throughout the country and are often accompanied with shows, musical events and sometimes foodtables.

India

In India, Goa with its inherent party culture, is the ideal venue for celebrating the birth of a new year. Tourists and backpackers from all over the world descend on Goa to revel in the festivities accompanying the New Year celebration. Most celebrations take place in the larger cities of India like Mumbai, Delhi, Pune, Bangalore, Chennai, Hyderabad, Kolkata, Ahmedabad and since 2009-10, in Chandigarh. Events such as live concerts and dances by Bollywood stars are organised and attended mostly by youngsters. Large crowds also gather at popular spots along the coastline such as the Gateway of India, Girgaum Chowpatty, Bandra Bandstand, Juhu Beach etc. More often than not friends rather than family tend to get together to celebrate the New Year.

Many people individually arrange "Puja's" of their respective gods and goddess(especially on 1 January) to mark the New Year.

Indonesia

The local government of Jakarta often holds a music show, a new year's countdown, and fireworks party in New Year's Eve celebration. The events often held in Monumen Nasional, Taman Impian Jaya Ancol, and Taman Mini Indonesia Indah. In Jakarta, people celebrates New Year's Eve in Jalan Muhammad Husni Thamrin, with their families, siblings, or their friends. Trumpet and fireworks are the most important things for Indonesian people to celebrate their New Year's Eve.

Ireland

The Irish call New Year's Eve *New Year's Eve*, or in Irish - *Oíche Chinn Bliana*, *Oíche na Coda Móire* or *Oíche Chaille*. Celebrations in major cities are modest. The beginning of 2009 was heralded only by the ringing of church bells. This is due to a ban on fireworks.

Italy

Italians call New Year's Eve *Capodanno* (the "head of the year") or *Notte di San Silvestro* (the night of St. Silvestro). Traditionally there are a set of rituals for the new year, such as wearing red underwear and getting rid of old or unused items by dropping them from the window, but this is and old tradition, followed by quite nobody today.

Dinner is often eaten with parents and friends. It often includes zampone or cotechino (a kind of spiced Italian sausage) and lentils. At half past eight pm, The President of the Republic reads a television message of greetings to Italians.

At midnight, fireworks are displayed across Italy.

Japan

Main article: Ōmisoka

The day is a preparation day to welcome *toshigami* (年神), new year's god. Therefore, traditionally, people clean their home and prepare Kadomatsu and/or Shimenawa to welcome the god before New Year's Eve.

Buddhist temples ring their bells 108 times at midnight. This tradition is called *joya no kane* (除夜の鐘) which means "bell rings on new year eve's night." The rings represent 108 elements of *bonō* (煩悩), defilements, or Kilesa in Sanskrit, which is said people have in their mind. The bells are rung to repent 108 of the *bonnō*.

A popular TV show on New Year's Eve in Japan is Red and White Year-end Song Festival. Kōhaku Uta Gassen is a 60-year-old tradition involving a singing contest between male and female teams of celebrity singers.

Kiribati, Republic of

This is the first country to receive the New Year. Kiritimati (UTC+14) is the first place of this country to see the sun rise.

Lebanon

In Lebanon, people celebrate the New Year's Eve by the use of fireworks, and by organizing tabouli, hummus and kibbi and other Lebanese foods for family and friend gatherings. These celebrations could also take place at some diners and clubs. Game shows are also organised where people can try their luck to win some money. The synchronised final countdown is broadcast through the leading TV channel and the celebrations usually continue until sunrise.

Malta

Malta organized its first street party in 2009, parallel to what other major countries in the world organize. The event was not highly advertised and controversial, due to the closing of an arterial street on the day.

Mexico

Mexicans down a grape with each of the twelve chimes of the bell during the New Year countdown, while making a wish with each one. On New Year's Eve, women who want to find love in the new year wear red underwear, or yellow if they want money. They make life-size dolls out of old clothes, fill them with fireworks and set them on fire at the stroke of midnight. Other traditions include sweeping the dirt out, taking luggage outside as a symbol of future trips, hanging sheep dolls (mainly made out of wool) in the doorknob for prosperity, among others. The celebrations are very similar to those of Spain.

Montenegro

Montenegrin New Year's Eve celebrations are held in all large cities on 1 January. These celebrations are usually accompanied by fireworks. It is usually celebrated together with family or friends in house or outside. Restaurants, clubs, cafe's and hotels are always organizing celebration with food and music.

Morocco

New Year's Eve is also celebrated in Morocco. Moroccans call it *Rass l'aam* or (رأس العام) which means the "head of the year".

Fireworks in New Year's Eve, Casablanca

In Casablanca, New Year's Eve is celebrated in the company of family and friends. People get together to eat cake, dance, laugh. Traditionally, people celebrate it at home, but some of them prefer to hit the clubs.

At midnight, fireworks are displayed across Ain Diab, in the Corniche of Casablanca.

Netherlands

New Year's Eve is called *Oud en Nieuw* ("Old and New") or simply *Oudejaarsavond* ("old year's evening"), and is usually celebrated as a cosy evening with family or friends. Traditional snack foods are *oliebollen* (oil dumplings) and *appelbeignets* (apple slice fritters). On television, the main feature is the *oudejaarsconference,* a performance by one of the major Dutch cabaretiers (comparable to stand-up comedy, but more serious; generally including a satirical review of the year's politics). In Reformed Protestant families, Psalm 90 is read, although this tradition is now fading away. At midnight, Glühwein *(bishopswine)* or Champagne is drunk. Many people fire off their own fireworks, which are on sale from a few days before; towns don't organise a central fireworks display. Public transport shuts down completely (the only scheduled time during the year) between approximately 20:00 and 01:00.

On television a clock is broadcast several minutes before midnight.

New Zealand

Gisborne is 496.3 kilometres (308.4 mi) west of the International Date Line and thus is the first major city to see the beginning of the new year, however it is Kiritimati, Republic of Kiribati that is the first "city" in the world to see the first sun rise for the year. In New Zealand, cities celebrate this with large street parties and fireworks displays. Elsewhere in New Zealand, local councils usually organise parties and street carnivals and fireworks displays. In recent years however, liquor bans have been imposed on many of the more popular areas due to disorder, vandalism and other anti-social behaviour. During the day of New Year's Eve, in recent years, the Black Caps have played a One Day International cricket game in Queenstown.

Philippines

Filipinos usually celebrate New Year's Eve with the company of family and close friends. Traditionally, most households stage a dinner party named *Media Noche* in their homes. Typical dishes include pancit, *Hamon* , Lechón (roasted pig), which is usually considered as the centerpiece of the dinner table. Barbecued food is also an integral part of the menu.

Most Filipinos follow a set of traditions that are typically observed during New Year's Eve. Included among these traditions is the customary habit of wearing clothes with circular patterns like polka dots, this signifies the belief that circles attract money and fortune or other colorful clothing to show enthusiasm for the coming year. Throwing coins at the stroke of midnight is said to increase wealth that year. Traditions also include the serving of circularly-shaped fruits, shaking of coins inside a metal casserole while walking around the house, and jumping up high which is believed to cause an increase in physical height. People also make loud noises by blowing on cardboard or plastic horns, called "*torotot*", banging on pots and pans or by igniting firecrackers and pyrotechnics at the stroke of midnight, in the belief that it scares away malevolent spirits and forces.

Urban areas are usually hosts to many New Year's Eve parties and countdown celebrations which are usually hosted by the private sector with the help of the local government. These parties usually display their own fireworks spectacles and are often very well attended.The main celebration is focused on Manila Bay at Roxas Boulevard, Manila Philippines.

Pakistan

New Year's Eve is usually celebrated in the country with joy; however, as Pakistan is an Islamic country, they also celebrate New Year's Eve on the every first of Muharram (First Islamic Month). It is celebrated as a religious occasion with Muslims offering special prayers on this eve.

Poland

The celebration of New Year's Eve in Poland is full of much vibrance. Traditionally, Poles have devoted each day on the calendar to a particular saint for adoration and devotion to that saint. December 31 is named after St. Sylvester, and thus the day is commonly referred to as "Sylvester". Celebrations partake both indoor and out, with the most notable being held in the Main Square - Rynek in Krakow. Here, thousands celebrate the New Year with live music and a fireworks display over St. Mary's Basilica. Similar festivities are held in cities around Poland such as Wrocław.

For those who do not wish to spend the New Year in a city, the mountains are a popular destination. Zakopane, located in the Carpathian Mountain Range, is the most popular Polish mountain resort.

Romania

The celebration of the New Year's Eve in Romania has a totally traditional flavor. Romanians welcome the New Year with the customs, rituals and conventions that have been around for centuries. The children as well as the adults, take part in the joyous celebrations with great enthusiasm. On New Year's Eve in Romania, small school going children sing Plugusorul and Sorcova. The songs wish good luck, happiness and success.

Russia

Most Russians celebrate New Year's Eve with their families and close friends. The celebration usually starts one or two hours before midnight and the common tradition is to "say farewell to the old year" by remembering most important events of the last twelve months. At five minutes to twelve most of the people watch the president's speech on TV or watch popular New Year TV shows ("Goluboy Ogonek"). There is a tradition to listen to the Kremlin clock bell ('Kuranty') ringing twelve times on the radio or on TV. During these last 12 seconds of the year people keep silence and make their secret wishes for the next year. After that they drink champagne and have rich dinner, watching TV concerts and having fun. Some people like starting fireworks outside and visiting their friends and neighbors. As the 30th and 31 December are working days, a lot of people also have small parties at work, though 31 December is mostly spent at home or with friends. There is an old superstition that if the first visitor (especially unexpected one) on the 1st of January is a man, the year will be good. People also try to start the new year without debts.

Serbia

New Year in Serbia is traditionally celebrated extensively. Indoors, families celebrate New Year's Eve with an abundance of food. Decorated "Christmas"-trees are predominantly related to New Year, hence called "novogodišnja (new years) jelka". Around or after midnight, "Deda Mraz" (Grandpa Frost) visits houses and leaves presents under the tree, to be unpacked then or, if the family is asleep, only to be discovered in the morning.

Restaurants, clubs, cafe's and hotels are usually full-booked and organize New Year's celebrations with food and live music.

However, Serbian New Year's celebrations are most known for the outdoors festivities in Belgrade, and several other major cities such as Novi Sad and Niš. As of mid-December, cities are extensively decorated and lit. The decorations remain until way into January due to the persistent influence of the old, Julian calendar. Throughout the region, especially amongst former Yugoslav republics, Belgrade is known as the place to be for major parties, concerts and happenings. It has become common for large groups of Slovenes to visit their former capital and celebrate the beginning of a new year. Especially since the mid-nineties, street celebrations grew into mass gatherings with hundreds of thousands of people, celebrating New Year on one of several locations throughout Belgrade. During former

President Milošević's mandate, the gatherings had a strong political connotation as well. As of 2000, every year the City of Belgrade organizes several concerts with major national and international performers on Belgrade's major squares; the Republic Square, Terazije Square and in front of the Serbian (formerly Federal) Parliament building. The concerts commence early in the evening and last well into the morning. Usually, there are separate celebrations and concerts organized for small children (Slavija Square) and for elderly (Kalemegdan park). Midnight is marked by major fireworks fired from suitable buildings within the city.

On January 1, the central Svetogorska street is closed for traffic and used to hold the "street of open heart" festival; food and warm drinks are served and open air theater plays are performed, while families with children as well as politicians (often including the President) walk down the street. The evening of the first of January is reserved for the so-called "repriza", a repetition of the previous night; people often go to the club, friends or square where they were last night to celebrate once more. Slightly down-scaled festivities are organized.

On January 13, a large part of the population celebrates "Serbian New Year", according to the Julian calendar. This time, usually one concert is organized in front of either City Hall or the National Parliament (in Belgrade), while fireworks are prepared by the Serbian Orthodox Church and fired from the Saint Sava Temple, where people also gather. Other cities also organize such celebrations.

Singapore

In Singapore, the biggest celebration and also the main focal point of all New Year's Eve celebrations in Singapore takes place at the Marina Bay area. It would be attended by some 250,000 or more people spanning around the bay area starting from the Marina Bay floating Stadium to the Esplanade promenade, the Esplanade Bridge, Benjamin Sheares Bridge, Merlion Park, and the Padang at City Hall facing the Marina Bay direction.

Other places where people has also soak in the celebration atmosphere in Marina Bay includes from nearby hotels such as The Fullerton Hotel, Marina Madarin, The Ritz-Carlton Millenia, Marina Bay Sands, offices located at Raffles Place, Marina Bay Financial Centre, Residential Apartments at The Sail @ Marina Bay, and from atop the world's tallest ferris wheel - The Singapore Flyer. All of whom are facing the Marina Bay direction and overlooking the waterfront also.

Out on the watersfronts of Marina Bay, 20,000 inflatable 'wishing spheres' - carrying 500,000 wishes penned down by Singaporeans would formed a visual arts display filled with brilliant colors beamed from the spotlights erected along the Esplanade promenade open area.

The audiences would also be entertained by a host of variety shows and concerts staged at the Marina Bay floating platform stage featuring local and overseas artistes viewable by all at the bay and telecast live on the republic's local TV channel.

10 seconds to the stroke of midnight, the concert emcees would be initiating the final countdown together with the audiences. And thereafter, spectacular and glittering fireworks would be fired off

from the waters at Marina Bay and lighting up the whole bay against the backdrop of the Singapore skyline.

Spain

Spanish New Year's Eve (*Nochevieja* or *Fin de Año* in Spanish, *Cap d'Any* in Catalan, *Cabo d'Anyo* in Aragonese) celebrations usually begin with a family dinner, traditionally including shrimp and lamb or capon. Spanish tradition says that wearing new, red underwear on New Year's Eve brings good luck. The actual countdown is primarily followed from the clock on top of the Casa de Correos building in Puerta del Sol square in Madrid. It is traditional to eat twelve grapes, one on each chime of the clock. This tradition has its origins in 1909, when grape growers in Alicante thought of it as a way

The *Puerta Del Sol* in 2005 New Year's Eve

to cut down on the large production surplus they had had that year. Nowadays, the tradition is followed by almost every Spaniard, and the twelve grapes have become synonymous with the New Year. After the clock has finished striking twelve, people greet each other and toast with sparkling wine such as cava or champagne, or alternatively with cider.

After the family dinner and the grapes, many young people attend New Year parties at pubs, discothèques and similar places (these parties are called *cotillones de nochevieja*, after the Spanish word *cotillón*, which refers to party supplies like confetti, party blowers, party hats, etc.). Parties usually last until the next morning and range from small, personal celebrations at local bars to huge parties with guests numbering the thousands at hotel convention rooms. Early next morning, party attendees usually gather to have the traditional winter breakfast of *chocolate con churros* (hot chocolate and fried pastry).

Suriname

Pagara (Red-firecracker-ribbons) New Year's Eve in Suriname is called Oud jaar which means old year. It is during this period that the Surinamese population goes to the city's commercial district to watch demonstrational fireworks. This is however, a spectacle based on the famous red-firecracker-ribbons. The bigger stores invest in these firecrackers and display them out in the streets. Every year the length of them is compared, and high praises are held for the company that has managed to import the largest ribbon. These celebrations start at 10 in the morning and finish the next day. The day is usually filled with laughter, dance, music, and drinking. When the night starts, the big street parties are already at full capacity. The most popular fiesta is the one that is held at café 't Vat in the main tourist district. The parties there stop between 10 and 11 at night. After which the people go home to light their pagaras (red-firecracker-ribbons) at midnight. After 12, the parties continue and the streets fill again until daybreak.

Switzerland

In Switzerland, New Year's Eve is typically celebrated at a residence with friends (Christmas usually having been celebrated with family). There are no particular main dishes associated with the event, although sweets and desserts are usual. Each commune has its own government-arranged countdown in a public space, accompanied with formal fireworks shows in larger cities.

Sweden

In Sweden, New Year's Eve is usually celebrated with families or with friends. A few hours before and after midnight, people usually party and eat a special dinner, often three courses. New Year's Eve is celebrated with large fireworks displays throughout the country, especially in the cities. People over 18 are allowed to buy fireworks, which are sold by local stores or by private persons. While watching or lighting up fireworks at midnight, people usually drink champagne. During the evening there is a showing on TV of the old West German cult classic *Dinner for One* with Freddie Frinton. This was released in 1963 in West Germany, Sweden 1969, and Denmark 1973.Ref: http://www.imdb.com/title/tt0121210/releaseinfo

Taiwan

Many people in Taiwan celebrate the end of the year. Concerts are held in most of the cities, including Taoyuan, Taichung, Taipei, and Kaoshiung. Recently, the nation has used higher technology to communicate among the cities via video, enabling the cities to count down together. The most crowded city is the capital, Taipei, where most people gather by Taipei 101 and shopping centres in its vicinity. The tower is located in the shopping and financial area of the Xinyi District. People gather around the streets of Taipei 101 as they count down. With each number they count, one of the layers of Taipei 101 (eight floors per layer) lights up until 0, when the fireworks shoot out from the top of each layer (eight layers excluding a layer under the antenna) in different directions, as shown in the picture at right.

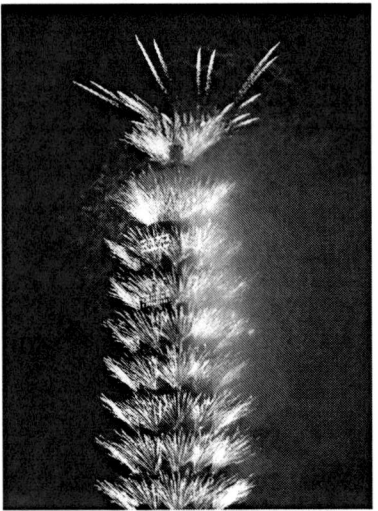

A fireworks display on Taipei 101, Taipei, Taiwan, New Year's 2008. A rare example of fireworks on a skyscraper.

Turkey

Numerous decorations and customs traditionally associated with Christmas and Bayrams find a secular translation in Turkish New Year's Eve celebrations, where homes and streets are lit up in glittering lights as well as various traditional Turkish aesthetic practices. Small gifts are exchanged, and large family dinners are organized with family and friends, featuring a special Zante currant-pimento-dill iç pilav dish, dolma, hot börek, baklava baklava and various other eggplant dishes, topped with warm pide, salep and boza.

Television and radio channels are known to continuously broadcast a variety of special New Year's Eve programs, while Municipalities all around the country organize fundraising events for the poor, in addition to celebratory public shows such as concerts and family-friendly events, as well as more traditional forms of entertainment such as the Karagöz and Hacivat shadow-theater and even performances by the Mehter - the Janissary Band that was founded during the days of the Ottoman Empire.

Public and private parties with large public attendances are organised in a number of cities and towns, particularly in the largest metropolitan areas such as Istanbul, Ankara, Izmir, Adana and Antalya, with the biggest celebrations taking place in Istanbul's Taksim, Beyoğlu, Nişantaşı and Kadıköy districts and Ankara's Kızılay Square, which generally feature dancing, concerts, laser and lightshows as well as the traditional countdown and fireworks display.

Ukraine

In the former Soviet Union, New Year has the same cultural significance as Christmas has in the United States, but without the religious connotations. Russian, Ukrainian and other families from former Soviet Union traditionally install spruce trees at home, the equivalent of a Christmas tree. In Eastern Europe, there is the Ded Moroz, who looks similar to Santa Claus, except he wears robes, and instead of reindeer, he is pulled by a *troika* (i.e. a three-horse drawn sled). Families gather to eat a large feast and reflect on the past year. They have a large celebration, make toasts, and make wishes for a happy New Year. Families give presents to their friends as well as informal acquaintances. This is due to Russians being a closely-knit community, and it is seen as a taboo to not give presents to those the family associates with. Children stay up until midnight, waiting for the New Year. Also, during these celebrations many Russians tune to special New Year shows, which have become a long-standing tradition for the Russian TV.

New Year is often considered a "pre-celebration" for the Eastern Orthodox living in Eastern Europe, primarily in Russia and Ukraine, since Christmas is celebrated on January 7 according to the Eastern Orthodox tradition.

United States

In the United States, New Year's Eve is a major social holiday. One of the top destination cities for New Year's Eve is New York City. Las Vegas's America's Party is also attracting a large number of New Year's Eve party goers with the famous Las Vegas Strip being closed to vehicles and fireworks launched from numerous rooftops.

Countdown 2006 in NYC

In the past 100 years the "ball dropping" on top of One Times Square in New York City, broadcast to all of America (and rebroadcast in many other countries), is a major component of the New Year celebration. The 11875-pound (5386 kg), 12-foot (3.7 m) diameter Waterford crystal ball located high above Times Square is lowered, starting at 11:59:00pm and reaching the bottom of its tower 60 seconds later, at the stroke of midnight (12:00:00am). This is repeated in many towns and cities across the United States. From 1981 to 1988, New York City dropped an enlarged apple in recognition of its nickname. It is sometimes referred to as "the big apple" like the city itself; the custom derives from the time signal that used to be given at noon in harbors.

From 1972 through 2007 (except in 1999), Dick Clark hosted televised coverage of the event called *Dick Clark's New Year's Rockin' Eve*, shown on ABC, and now renamed *Dick Clark's New Year's Rockin' Eve with Ryan Seacrest* for the arrival of 2009 with Ryan Seacrest handling hosting duties. The show did not air for the arrival of 2000 as it was preempted by *ABC 2000 Today*, but Dick Clark reported during the "ABC 2000" broadcast, with an introduction from Peter Jennings, saying some would not consider it the New Year if Dick Clark did not

Excessive drinking is longstanding feature of U.S. New Year's Eve celebrations (1912 postcard).

count it down. From 1956 to 1976 on CBS, Guy Lombardo and his Royal Canadians serenaded the United States from the ballroom of the Waldorf-Astoria Hotel on Park Avenue in New York City. The Royal Canadians continued on CBS until 1978, and ***Happy New Year, America*** replaced it in 1979, continuing until 1995. The song Auld Lang Syne has become a popular song to sing at midnight on New Year's Eve, with the Lombardo version being the standard. NBC also has hosted New Year's coverage; traditionally, the networks' late night hosts have hosted special editions of their regular shows (including a special Central Time Zone-specific countdown on *Late Night with Conan O'Brien*), but since 2005, the network has opted for a special entitled *New Year's Eve with Carson Daly*. Fox, CNN, and Fox News Channel also have their own New Year's specials. One of the more popular traditions is the Twilight Zone marathon hosted on SyFy (formerly SciFi)

Communities

Religious Communities

United Methodists and Protestant churches serving the black community have a tradition of New Year's Eve known as "Watch Night." The faithful congregate in worship services commencing New Year's Eve night and continuing past midnight into the new year. Watch Night is a time for giving thanks for the blessings of the outgoing year and praying for divine favor during the upcoming year. Though held by some to have begun in the African American community, watch night can actually be traced back to John Wesley, the founder of Methodism. Wesley learned the custom of Watchnight from the Moravian Brethren who came to England in the 1730s. Moravian Congregations still observe the Watchnight Service on New year's Eve. Watch Night took on special significance to African Americans on New Year's Eve 1862, however, as slaves anticipated the arrival of January 1, 1863, and Lincoln's signing of the Emancipation Proclamation.

Local celebrations

Many cities in the US have their own local version of the celebration, even while keeping an eye on New York, and the New York-centric aspect of the holiday is diminishing.

In recent years, festivities in downtown Cleveland, Ohio have increased in popularity, demonstrating a midwest style to the traditional New Year's festivities. Specifically, several bars including "Blind Pig" and more recently "Cadillac Ranch" host parties drawing thousands of revelers. The party at "Cadillac Ranch" is especially a sign of the revitalization of the Cleveland area as its location is adjacent to the Health Line.

Many cities, echoing the New York tradition of ball drop, also descend or lower an object (or an enlarged representation of an object) For example, big balloon drops are traditional at the Professionals Guild singles New Year's Eve parties in Sacramento and in the San Francisco Bay Area.

The festivities in downtown Chicago take place at Navy Pier, as fireworks are shot off next to the pier.

In some communities the objects dropped have special local significance. Orange County, California, Orange County, Texas, and Orange County, New York, all drop large oranges (Orange County, Florida, tried it briefly, but has since ceased doing so). There are also examples of things going up. In Seattle the countdown is done by raising the Space Needle's elevator and launching fireworks up the side of the tower until both reach the top at midnight. Also Atlanta, Georgia does their famous Peach Drop, another event that is shown on *Dick Clark's New Year's Rockin' Eve*.

Further information: List of objects dropped on New Year's Eve

New Year's Eve is a major event in Las Vegas, Nevada, where the Las Vegas Strip is shut down as several hundred thousand people party. New Year's Eve is traditionally the busiest day of the year at Walt Disney World in Florida and Disneyland in California, where the parks stay open late and the usual nightly fireworks are supplemented by an additional New Year's Eve-specific show at midnight. In New Orleans, Louisiana, another of the most popular New Year celebration venues in North America, similar crowds of hundreds of thousands gather in the French Quarter, particularly on Bourbon Street and Canal Street, to celebrate the New Year.

Many cities also celebrate First Night, a non-alcohol family-friendly New Year's Celebration, generally featuring performing artists, community events, parades, and fireworks displays. First Night began in Boston in 1976 and is now found in over 60 cities nationwide. A similar celebration is Providence, Rhode Island's Bright Night, and an artist-run arts celebration that started when Providence's First Night went bankrupt in 2003.

Celebratory gunfire and unapproved fireworks use

In several cities of the U.S., New Year celebrations are punctuated by celebratory gunfire which could potentially cause injuries or deaths. Police departments in many cities, aided by gun safety organizations, have attempted to crack down on this practice through technology and stiffer penalties.

Venezuela

In Venezuela, many of the traditions are very similar to the ones from Spain, with an over-emphasis in traditions that supposedly will bring good luck in the year forthcoming. Those who want to find love in the New Year are supposed to wear red underwear on New Year's Eve; those who want money must have a bill of high value when toast, those who want to travel must go out home while carrying some luggage, and so on. Yellow underwear is worn to bring happiness in the New Year.

Usually, people listen to radio specials, which give a countdown and announce the New Year according to the legal hour in Venezuela, and, in Caracas, following the twelve bells from the Cathedral of Caracas. During these special programs is a tradition to broadcast songs about the sadness on the end of the year, being popular favorites "Viejo año" ("Old year") by Gaita group Maracaibo 15 and "Cinco pa' las 12" ("Five minutes before twelve") who was versioned by several popular singers like Nestor Zavarce, Nancy Ramos and José Luis Rodríguez El Puma, and the unofficial hymn for the first minutes of the New Year is "Año Nuevo, Vida Nueva" ("New Year, New Life"), by the band Billo's Caracas Boys.

Songs

In English-speaking countries, a few popular songs are associated with New Year's Eve and it is common to hear them on the radio these countries on, or shortly before, December 31.

- "Auld Lang Syne" (a Scottish folk song written by Robert Burns, the song most closely associated with the holiday)
- "Let's Start the New Year Right" from *Holiday Inn* by Bing Crosby.
- "It Was a Very Good Year" by Frank Sinatra.
- "It's Just Another New Year's Eve" by Barry Manilow.
- "What Are You Doing New Year's Eve?" recorded by various singers, most of them female.
- "Same Old Lang Syne" by Dan Fogelberg
- "Happy New Year" by ABBA
- "The New Year" by Death Cab For Cutie
- "A Long December" by Counting Crows
- "New Year's Eve" by The Walkmen
- "New Year's Day" by U2
- "What a Wonderful World" by Louis Armstrong
- "Maybe Baby (New Year's Day)" by Sugarland

Year 2000 related songs

During the festivities for the year 2000, Prince's *1999* was re-released and enjoyed increased popularity due to the song's namesake year. Will Smith also released a song entitled Will 2K, which also proved successful, owing to the lyrics' celebration of millennium parties. Robbie Williams enjoyed a similar success with his 1998 single *Millennium*, as did Pulp for their 1995 song Disco 2000.

Staying at home

While many people go to parties to celebrate New Year's Eve, according to a recent survey, 62% stay at home. Seven percent do not celebrate New Year's Eve at all, though a proportion of those may well tune in to the live tv broadcasts from the comfort of their homes.

See also

- Áramótaskaupið in Iceland
- New Year
- Chinese New Year
- Hogmanay Live
- Nowruz, the Persian New Year
- Malanka, a Ukrainian holiday

External links

- Youtube: PyroAndMore [1] a Fireworks Video

Birthday

A **birthday**, as the term implies, is the day or anniversary of the particular day on which a person was born. Though by no means universal, birthdays are celebrated in numerous cultures, often with a party or, in some instances, a rite of passage. Though major religious traditions such as the Buddhist or the Christian celebrate the birth of their founders, the most prominent example of which is Christmas, principled opposition to the very idea of celebrating birthdays is to be found among certain religious groups.

Candles spell out the traditional English birthday greeting

A girl on her 18th birthday.

Cultural and legal conventions

In most legal systems, one becomes a legal adult on a particular birthday (often 14th through 21st), and at different ages gains different rights and responsibilities – voting, certain drug use (for example, alcohol, purchasing tobacco), eligibility for military conscription or voluntary enlistment, purchasing lottery tickets, obtaining vehicle driving licenses, etc.

Many cultures have one or more coming of age birthdays:

- Jewish boys become bar mitzvah on their 13th birthday. Jewish girls become bat mitzvah on their 12th birthday, or sometimes on their 13th birthday in Reform and Conservative Judaism.
- In Hispanic-American countries the *quinceañera* celebration traditionally marks a girl's 15th birthday.

- In Indian Hindus, the 12th or 13th birthday is replaced with a grand "thread ceremony." The child takes a blessed thread and wears it, symbolizing his coming of age. This ceremony is practiced amongst boys in the Hindu Brahmin culture.

- In the Philippines, girls on their 18th birthday or boys on their 21st birthday celebrate a debut.

- In some Asian countries that follow the Zodiac calendar, there is a tradition of celebrating the 60th birthday.

The birthdays of historically significant people, like national heroes or founders, are often commemorated by an official holiday. Some saints are remembered by a liturgical feast (sometimes on a presumed birthday). By analogy, the Latin term *Dies natalis* is applied to the anniversary of an institution (such as a university).

A person's Golden or Grand Birthday, also referred to as their "Lucky Birthday", "Champagne Birthday" or "Star Birthday", occurs when they turn the age of their birth day (e.g., when someone born on the 25th of the month turns 25).

Name days

In some Roman Catholic and Eastern Orthodox countries such as Spain, France, Poland, Russia, Romania, Bulgaria, Slovakia, Czech Republic, Hungary, or Greece and Latvia it is common to have a 'name day'/'Saint's day'. It's common in Latin America too. This is celebrated in much the same way as a birthday, but is held on the official day of a saint with the same Christian name as the birthday person; the difference being that one may look up a person's name day in a calendar, or easily remember common name days (for example, *John* or *Mary*); however in pious traditions, the two were often made to concur by giving a newborn the name of a saint celebrated on its birthday, or even the name of a feast, for example, *Noel* or *Pascal* (French for Christmas and "of Easter"); for one, Togliatti got *Palmiro* as first name because he was born on Palm Sunday.

Monthly birthdays

It is not uncommon for parents to track their child's age using months Child development stages. This is logical, since there is such tremendous development from one month to the next for children under two years in age. After this point the most common tradition is to celebrate birthdays annually. Recently, in an effort to consciously move away from the stigma of age and simultaneously celebrate daily life, a new trend has developed to celebrate Monthly Birthdays.

Annual Birthdays are typically a celebration of the individual, often with a group gathering to focus attention on the birthday boy or girl. In contrast, Monthly Birthdays are about seizing the day. "Monthlies," as they are often called, are a reminder to enjoy life, and take advantage of all the great things around you.

Monthly birthdays also give you the added benefit of excellent numerology. Specific attention is typically focused on base-ten graduations, but creative types prefer interesting number patterns such as 111, 321 ("3, 2, 1 Blast-off Birthday"), 327 (3 cubed is equal to 27), and so on. Additionally, little cultural stigma is placed on monthly numbers, and therefore is seen as less stressful (360th monthly vs 30 years).

Official birthdays

Some notables, particularly monarchs, have an *official birthday* on a fixed day of the year, which may not necessarily match their actual birthday, but on which celebrations are held. Examples are:

- Jesus Christ's traditional birthday is celebrated as Christmas Day around the world, on December 25. As some Eastern churches use the Julian calendar, December 25 will fall upon January 7 in the Gregorian calendar.

- The Queen's Official Birthday in Australia, Fiji, New Zealand, as well as the United Kingdom; in Canada, this day is known as Victoria Day.

- The Grand Duke's Official Birthday in Luxembourg is typically celebrated upon June 23.

- *Koninginnedag* in the Kingdom of the Netherlands is typically celebrated upon

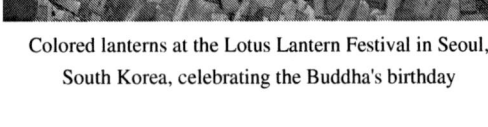
Colored lanterns at the Lotus Lantern Festival in Seoul, South Korea, celebrating the Buddha's birthday

April 30. Queen Beatrix fixed it at the birthday of her mother, the previous Queen, to avoid the winter weather associated with her own birthday in January.

- The Current Japanese Emperor Heisei (Akihito)'s birthday is December 23, which is a national holiday in Japan.

- The previous Japanese Emperor Showa (Hirohito)'s birthday was April 29. After his death, the holiday was kept as "Showa no Hi", or "Showa Day". This holiday falls close to Golden Week, the week in late April and early May that contains several national holidays and is a popular week-long vacation for many workers in Japan.

While it is uncommon to have an official holiday for a head of state's birthday in a republic, this does occur; for example, George Washington's birthday in the United States, which is commonly called Presidents Day.

Frequency

According to a public record births database, birthdays in the United States are quite evenly distributed for the most part. However, there tend to be more births in September and October. This may be because there is holiday season nine months before, or from the fact that the longest nights of the year happen in the Northern Hemisphere nine months before as well. October 5 is considered to be the most populous birthday in the United States.

Timezones and birthdays

A person's birthday is usually recorded according to the time zone of the place of birth. Thus people born in Samoa at 11:30 pm will record their birthdate as one day before Coordinated Universal Time (UTC) and those born in the Line Islands will record their birthdate one day after UTC. They will apparently be born two days apart, while some of the apparently older ones may be younger in hours. Those who live in different time zones from their birth often exclusively celebrate their birthdays at the local time zone. In addition, the intervention of Daylight Saving Time can result in a case where a baby born second being recorded as having been born up to an hour before their predecessor.

Leap day

> *See: Leapling and February 29 #Births*

Religious opposition

Judaism

In Judaism, the perspective on birthday celebrations is disputed by various rabbis. In the Hebrew Bible, the one single mention of a celebration being held in commemoration of someone's day of birth is for the Egyptian Pharaoh. In addition, in the Greek Scriptures, King Herod beheaded a Christian, John the Baptizer, at his birthday celebration. On the other hand angels and shepherds celebrated the day of birth of Jesus Christ, and by reading first Job 1:3 and then Job 3:1, 3 it is seen that the children of righteous Job had special banquets for their days of birth.

The bar mitzvah of 13-year-old Jewish boys, or bat mitzvah for 12-year-old Jewish girls, is perhaps the only Jewish celebration undertaken in what is often perceived to be in coalition with a birthday. However, the essence of a bar/bat mitzvah celebration is entirely religious in origin (i.e. the attainment of religious maturity according to Jewish law) and not secular, despite modern celebrations where the secular "birthday" element often overshadows the essence of it as a religious rite. With or without the "birthday" celebration, the child nevertheless becomes a bar or bat mitzvah, and the celebration can be on that day or any date after it. In Jewish tradition, it is said that the person making a birthday cake can not also be the person celebrating the birthday, or they may bring a year of bad luck to their family

Christianity

The early Christians did not celebrate Christ's birth because they considered the celebration of anyone's birth to be a pagan custom. Few branches of Christianity today hold an official stance on birthdays. Orthodox Christianity prefers the celebration of name days only, though not for theological reasons. Some Christian communities, especially in the Hispanosphere, celebrate both naming days and birthdays. Jehovah's Witnesses and some Sacred Name groups refrain from celebrating birthdays on the basis that they are portrayed in a negative light in the Bible and have historical connections with magic, superstitions, and Paganism.

Superstitious origins of celebrations

A number of possible superstitious origins for customs associated with birthday celebrations have been suggested. One source states that the tradition of birthday parties started in Europe. It was feared that evil spirits were particularly attracted to people on their birthdays and to protect them, they would be visited by friends and family, who would bring good thoughts and wishes.

See also

- Various birthdays are mentioned on the pages devoted to each day of the year, from January 1 to December 31.
- Birthday paradox
- Birthday attack
- East Asian age reckoning - a different method of age reckoning to birthdays that is used in some Asian countries.
- Half-birthday
- Death anniversary/ Yahrzeit
- Unbirthday
- Decimal Birthday
- Sashtiabdhapoorthi
- Birthstones

Further reading

- Curtis Regan, Dian (March 1991). *The Class With the Summer Birthdays*. Henry Holth & Co. ISBN 978-0805016574.

Homecoming

Homecoming is the tradition of welcoming back former residents and alumni of an institution. It most commonly refers to a tradition in many universities, colleges and high schools in North America. It usually includes activities for students and alumni, such as sports and culture events and a parade through the streets of the city or town. Additionally, the term can also refer to the special services conducted by some religious congregations, particularly by many smaller American Protestant churches, that are often held annually but sometimes as one-time-only events, to celebrate church heritage and welcome back former members or pastors.

United States

Homecoming is an annual tradition of the United States. People, towns, high schools and colleges come together, usually in late September or early October, to welcome back former residents and alumni. It is built around a central event, such as a banquet and, most often, a game of American football, or, on occasion, basketball, ice hockey or soccer. When celebrated by schools, the activities vary widely. However, they usually consist of a football game played on a school's home football field, activities for students and alumni, a parade featuring the school's marching band and sports teams, and the coronation of a Homecoming Queen (and at many schools, a Homecoming King). A dance commonly follows the game.

Origins

The tradition of Homecoming has its origins in alumni football games held at colleges and universities since the mid-19th century. Many schools lay claim to having the first Homecoming, but several seem to have the strongest claims. The NCAA, Trivial Pursuit, and Jeopardy! give the title to the University of Missouri's 1911 football game during which alumni were encouraged to attend.

The history of the University of Missouri Homecoming can be traced back to 1891, when the Missouri Tigers first faced off against the Kansas Jayhawks in football in the first installment of the Border War, which is also the oldest college football rivalry west of the Mississippi River. The intense rivalry originally took place at neutral sites, usually in Kansas City, Missouri, until a new conference regulation was announced that required intercollegiate football games to be played on collegiate campuses. To renew excitement in the rivalry, ensure adequate attendance at the new location, and celebrate the first meeting of the two teams on the Mizzou campus in Columbia, Missouri, Mizzou

Athletic Director Chester Brewer invited all alumni to "come home" for the game in 1911. Along with the football game, the celebration included a parade and spirit rally with bonfire. The event was a success, with nearly 10,000 alumni coming home to take part in the celebration and watch the Tigers and Jayhawks play to a 3-3 tie. The Missouri homecoming model, with its parade and spirit rally centered around a large football game is the model that has gone on to take hold at colleges and high schools across the United States.

Baylor University and The University of Illinois at Urbana-Champaign both held events similar to modern homecomings in 1909 and 1910, respectively. All of these events had homecoming-like characteristics such as a football game, visiting alumni, and a parade. It's likely that the traditions at these schools and others merged and spread nationwide. By the 1920s homecoming was widely celebrated across the nation.

In 1909, Baylor University held an organized alumni event described as a "Home-Coming" whose focus point was a varsity sports match, as well as a concert, pep rally, parade, and bonfire; however, the extensively planned event was isolated and wasn't replicated again at Baylor until 1915.

The University of Illinois at Urbana-Champaign credits two senior members of the class of 1910 with establishing the tradition of homecoming at Illinois. These two men were Clarence F. Williams and W. Elmer Ekblaw. According to recollections Williams in 1930, the idea came to the two men in 1910 while they were sitting on the steps of the YMCA discussing ways of contributing to their alma mater. The men's idea culminated in Illinois' first homecoming event on October 15, 1910. The event celebration centered around the football game against the University of Chicago, and it also included various alumni reunions, initiations, and banquets.

Traditions

Homecoming Court

The Homecoming Court is a representative group of students that, in a coeducational institution, consists of a King and Queen, and possibly Prince(s) and Princess(es). In a single-sex institution, the Homecoming Court will usually consist of only a King and Princes (for a male school) or a Queen and Princesses (for a female school), although some schools may choose to join with single-gender schools of the opposite gender to elect the Homecoming Court jointly.

Generally, the King and Queen are students completing their final years of study at their school (also called seniors), while the Prince and Princess are underclassmen. In high school, 17- or 18-year-old students in their final year are represented by a King or Queen; in college, students who are completing their final year of study, usually between 21 and 23 years old.

Classmates traditionally nominate students who have done a lot to contribute to their school, then students vote for members of the Court from the nominees. Once the Homecoming Court candidates are announced, the entire student body votes for the Queen and King. The voting is often conducted by secret ballot, but other methods may also be used by certain schools.

Local rules determine when the Homecoming Queen and King are crowned. Sometimes, the big announcement comes at a pep rally, school assembly, or public ceremony one or more days before the game. Other schools crown their royalty at the Homecoming football game, a dance or other school event.

Often, the previous year's Queen and King are invited back to crown their successors. If they are absent for whatever reason, someone else − usually, another previous Queen or King, a popular teacher, or other designated person − will perform those duties. Usually, the Queen is crowned first, followed by the King. The crowning method also varies by school.

Homecoming court members who are not crowned king or queen are often called escorts or royalty . They are often expected to participate in the week's activities as well. At some schools, a Homecoming Prince/Princess, Duke/Duchess etc. (often underclassmen nominated by their classmates) are crowned along with the King and Queen; sometimes, middle school and junior high students may partake in the high school activities.

As of late, less and less schools have a Homecoming Court. Due to bullying, harassment, and other issues that have negative effects that tend to divide the school (being against the spirit of Homecoming), often the students choose to eliminate the Court altogether. Other times though when the Student Governments do not step in authorities such as school boards will cancel the Homecoming Court.

Parade

Many Homecoming celebrations include a parade. Students often select the grand marshal based on his/her service and support to the school and/or community. The parade includes the school's marching band and different school organizations floats created by the classes and organizations and most of the sports get a chance to be in the parade. Every class prepares a float which corresponds with the Homecoming theme or related theme of school spirit as assign by school administrators. In addition, the Homecoming Court takes part in the parade, often riding together in one or more convertibles as part of the parade. The parade is often part of a series of activities scheduled for that specific day, which can also include a pep rally, bonfire, snake dance, and other activities for students and alumni.

Tailgate

At most major colleges and universities, the football game and preceding tailgate are the most widely recognized and heavily attended events of the week. Alumni gather from all around the world to return to their Alma Mater and reconnect with one another and take part in the festivities. Students, alumni, businesses, and members of the community set up tents in parking lots, fields, and streets near the stadium to cook out, play games, socialize, binge drink, and even enjoy live music in many instances. These celebrations often last straight through the game for those who do not have tickets but still come to take part in the socializing and excitement of the homecoming atmosphere. Most tents even include television or radio feeds of the game for those without tickets.

Picnic

Sometimes during the school week, a picnic could occur. The picnic is very similar to the tailgate party, but it occurs after school or during the school's lunch period.

Dress-up days

Throughout the week, many schools (particularly high schools) engage in special dress-up days, sometimes called "Spirit Week", where students are allowed to wear clothing suitable to the theme (e.g., toga day, cowboy day, nerd day, pirate day, Rat Pack Day) leading to the homecoming. Students traditionally wear clothing with their school's name, or clothing and makeup of their school's colors on Friday.

Mums

A tradition that has been in place for almost a century at many Southwestern American high schools, especially in Texas, homecoming dates exchange mums and garters on Homecoming Friday, to wear to school and then to the big game, while at some smaller schools students where them to the dance this is usually not the norm. These are very elaborate corsages (for the girls, usually pinned to clothing on the chest or shoulder) or garters (for the boys, worn on the arm) that consist of large flowers, they come in several sizes and shapes and the larger the better, (usually a white synthetic chrysanthemum) surrounded by a ribbon ruffle. Long ribbons, decorations and trinkets and bells are hung from the mum. These decorations are carefully chosen to indicate the students' class, homecoming date, activities, and interests, in addition to commemorating the homecoming event with decorations related to the school and the homecoming game.

Riots

Occasionally, students at various high schools or colleges have engaged in violent or destructive riots. Common rioting activities include the burning of furniture or cars, rallying noisily in the streets, hazing (throwing pennies/attacking freshmen) and/or vandalizing the school of the opponents. Schools generally denounce these activities.

Rallies

Many schools hold a rally during Homecoming week, often one or more nights before the game. The events vary, but may include skits, games, introduction of the homecoming court (and coronation of the King and Queen if that is the school's tradition), and comments from the football players and/or coach about the upcoming game.

At some schools, the Homecoming rally ends with a bonfire (in which old wood structures, the rival school's memorabilia and other items are burned in a controlled fire.) Many colleges and high schools no longer hold bonfires because of accidents that have occurred surrounding these events in the past. The most well known accident took place in 1999, when 12 students were killed and 27 others were injured at Texas A&M University when a 40-foot-tall (12 m) pile of logs that had been assembled for a homecoming bonfire collapsed.

Homecoming dance

The Homecoming Dance – usually the culminating event of the week (for high schools) – is a formal or informal event, either at the school or an off-campus location. The venue is decorated, and either a disc jockey or band is hired to play music. In many ways, it is a fall prom. Homecoming dances could be informal as well just like standard school dances. At high schools, the homecoming dances are sometimes held in the high school gymnasium or outside in a large field.

Since most colleges are too large to facilitate a campus-wide dance, these events are usually handled instead by student organizations such as fraternities, sororities, and residential colleges. Because football and alumni events are the focal points of collegiate homecoming, dances often take place during a different week when schedules are more permitting, or not at all.

Competitions

While at the high school level, students generally compete by grade level in events such as the spirit days and parade floats, the competition at the collegiate level is mainly between Greek-letter organizations and, to a lesser degree, residence halls. At most larger schools, fraternities and sororities compete on parade floats, house decorations, skits, talent competitions, and even service events such as blood drives or food drives. Sometimes on coronation night, some schools have games that they play between classes. Such events include the pyramid, the 3 legged race, the pop chug, and tug of war.

Smaller school homecomings

While most schools schedule their Homecoming activities around football, smaller schools that do not field a football team may plan the annual event at another time of the year. In these instances, basketball, ice hockey or soccer serves as the "big game" for students and alumni. Often in smaller towns with smaller populations, the parade is omitted.

At schools without athletic programs, the centerpiece event is usually a banquet, where alumni are recognized. This format is also used for alumni events of high schools that have either closed or consolidated with other high schools; the high school classes continue to meet and celebrate their years at their now-defunct alma mater.

Courtwarming

In some parts of the country, high school basketball has gained a homecoming celebration of its own. Often referred to as *Winter Homecoming*, *Hoopcoming*, *Coronation*, *Snowcoming*, or *Courtwarming* (the latter is especially prominent in parts of Missouri), it usually includes rallies, dress-up days, special dinners, king and queen coronations, and other winter-friendly activities typically associated with football homecoming.

Similar events

Some schools have Homecoming-like events during the school year. Many of them have similar traditions to homecoming events such as the big game, dress up days, dance, etc.

Outside the U.S.

Canada

Homecoming celebrations are uncommon at universities across Canada. The best-known and largest homecoming weekends are held by UOIT, University of Western Ontario, McMaster University, Queen's University, Trent University, University of Waterloo and Wilfrid Laurier University each year. Canadian homecoming weekends are often centred around a football game but are also filled with events such as "pancake keggers" and parades.

In Newfoundland and Labrador, communities have a "Come Home Year" where people who have moved away from their town come back from across Canada. In 2000, there was a provincial "Come Home Year", where many people came back to visit their various communities.

Homecomings are not popular among Canadian high schools, and it is rare to find one that celebrates homecoming. Newmarket High School, London South Collegiate Institute and Earl Haig Secondary School are the only known schools in Ontario to arrange homecomings[citation needed]. Upper Canada College also has a longstanding homecoming tradition, although it calls the event A-Day (Association Day).

Other

The term "homecoming" can also refer to the special services conducted by some religious congregations, particularly by many smaller American Protestant churches, to celebrate church heritage and welcome back former members or pastors. They are often held annually, but are sometimes held as one-time-only events, to celebrate the occasion.

Homecoming should not be confused with prom, as they usually occur at different times of the year. Homecoming usually occurs in the fall, and prom usually occurs in the spring.

See also

- Prom
- Winter Formal

References

Notes

Article Sources and Contributors

House party *Source*: http://en.wikipedia.org/?oldid=388455790 *Contributors*: Closedmouth

Distilled beverage *Source*: http://en.wikipedia.org/?oldid=389846906 *Contributors*: 1 anonymous edits

Beer *Source*: http://en.wikipedia.org/?oldid=387511505 *Contributors*: Rich Farmbrough

Wine *Source*: http://en.wikipedia.org/?oldid=390586018 *Contributors*:

Cocktail *Source*: http://en.wikipedia.org/?oldid=384847767 *Contributors*: Wahrmund

Keg stand *Source*: http://en.wikipedia.org/?oldid=383065391 *Contributors*: 1 anonymous edits

Drinking game *Source*: http://en.wikipedia.org/?oldid=390499831 *Contributors*: E-Kartoffel

Funnel *Source*: http://en.wikipedia.org/?oldid=390074073 *Contributors*: Andy Dingley

Shotgunning *Source*: http://en.wikipedia.org/?oldid=388663144 *Contributors*:

Never have I ever *Source*: http://en.wikipedia.org/?oldid=388001724 *Contributors*: Tilla

Pennying *Source*: http://en.wikipedia.org/?oldid=387968905 *Contributors*:

Beer pong *Source*: http://en.wikipedia.org/?oldid=390645222 *Contributors*: Charwinger21

Beerdarts *Source*: http://en.wikipedia.org/?oldid=379883503 *Contributors*: PHermans

Kings (card game) *Source*: http://en.wikipedia.org/?oldid=389853161 *Contributors*: 1 anonymous edits

Pizza *Source*: http://en.wikipedia.org/?oldid=388779268 *Contributors*: Ohnoitsjamie

Potato chip *Source*: http://en.wikipedia.org/?oldid=390667538 *Contributors*: 1 anonymous edits

Disc jockey *Source*: http://en.wikipedia.org/?oldid=390560948 *Contributors*: Binksternet

Dance *Source*: http://en.wikipedia.org/?oldid=390141859 *Contributors*:

Saint Patrick's Day *Source*: http://en.wikipedia.org/?oldid=390525504 *Contributors*: Ohnoitsjamie

New Year's Eve *Source*: http://en.wikipedia.org/?oldid=390045933 *Contributors*: 1 anonymous edits

Birthday *Source*: http://en.wikipedia.org/?oldid=390443982 *Contributors*: Île flottante

Homecoming *Source*: http://en.wikipedia.org/?oldid=390629063 *Contributors*: 1 anonymous edits

Image Sources, Licenses and Contributors

CPSIA information can be obtained at www.ICGtesting.com
Printed in the USA
LVOW052104271111

256679LV00003B/151/P